Old English Poetry

Published under the auspices of the
CENTER FOR MEDIEVAL AND RENAISSANCE STUDIES
University of California, Los Angeles

Contributions of the

UCLA CENTER FOR MEDIEVAL AND RENAISSANCE STUDIES

1. Medieval Secular Literature. William Matthews, editor

2. Galileo Reappraised. Carlo L. Golino, editor

3. The Transformation of the Roman World—Gibbon's Problem after Two Centuries. Lynn White, jr., editor

4. Scientific Methods in Medieval Archaeology. Rainer Berger, editor

5. Violence and Civil Disorder in Italian Cities, 1200–1500. Lauro Martines, editor

6. The Darker Vision of the Renaissance. Robert S. Kinsman, editor

7. The Copernican Achievement. Robert S. Westman, editor

8. First Images of America: The Impact of the New World on the Old. Fredi Chiappelli, editor; Michael J. B. Allen and Robert L. Benson, co-editors

9. Friedrich Diez Centennial Lectures. Edward F. Tuttle, editor (Supplement to *Romance Philology*, vol. XXX, no. 2, 1976)

10. Old English Poetry: Essays on Style. Daniel G. Calder, editor

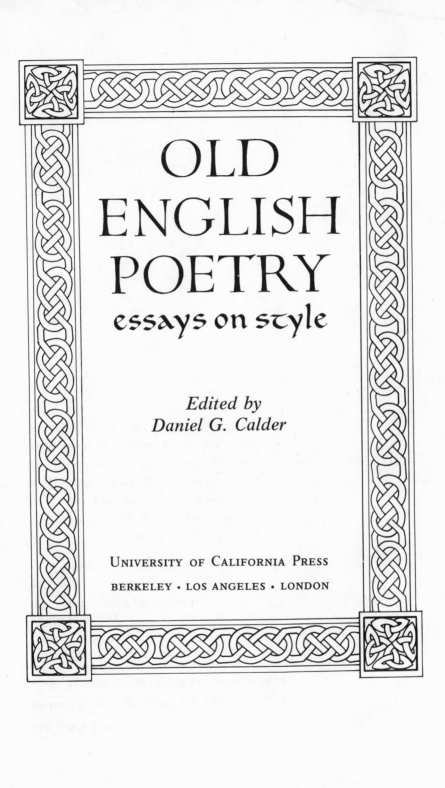

OLD ENGLISH POETRY

essays on style

Edited by
Daniel G. Calder

UNIVERSITY OF CALIFORNIA PRESS

BERKELEY · LOS ANGELES · LONDON

The emblem of the Center for Medieval and
Renaissance Studies reproduces the imperial
eagle of the gold *augustalis* struck after 1231 by
Emperor Frederick II; Elvira and Vladimir
Clain-Stefanelli, *The Beauty and Lore of Coins.
Currency and Medals* (Croton-on-Hudson,
1974), fig. 130 and p. 106.

University of California Press
Berkeley and Los Angeles, California

University of California Press, Ltd.
London, England

Copyright © 1979
by The Regents of the University of California
ISBN: 0-520-03830-4
Library of Congress Catalog Card Number: 78-65473

Printed in the United States of America

1 2 3 4 5 6 7 8 9

CONTENTS

ACKNOWLEDGMENTS

With the exception of my historical survey, these essays are based on papers delivered at a symposium on Old English poetry held in Los Angeles, March 31 to April 2, 1977. The symposium was co-sponsored by the Center for Medieval and Renaissance Studies and the Department of English. I am especially grateful to the Center's Director, Professor Fredi Chiappelli, for his professional and personal support, and to the Chairman of the English Department, Professor Peter Thorslev, Jr. The Graduate Division of UCLA also provided a generous subsidy and I would like to extend my appreciation to James E. Phillips, Dean of the Graduate Division. Many people worked very hard in preparing both the conference and this book: Thomas Bandy, Robert Bjork, Abigail Bok, John Chittenden, Hana Hrabec, Carol D. Lanham, Carol Pasternack and Harriet Woolf deserve much of the credit for whatever success this enterprise may have. My special thanks to Jeanette Gilkison who typed more than one draft of this manuscript.

D.G.C.

Los Angeles, California
February 22, 1978

vii

THE STUDY OF STYLE
IN OLD ENGLISH POETRY:
A HISTORICAL INTRODUCTION

Daniel G. Calder

THE OLD ENGLISH poetic tradition remained intact for centuries. While some minor changes did occur, the basic principles of this strongly conservative style scarcely altered. Thus Romantic notions of "The Poet" offer no help in explicating these largely anonymous and formulaic poems, because their impersonality and remoteness call attention to style without reference to biography. In Old English poetry style is not the man himself, as Shippey reminds us (Shippey 1972, 13). Indeed some modern criticism entirely ignores the question of an author's psychology in matters of style. Richard Ohmann, for example, writes, "A style is a *way* of doing *it*" (Ohmann 1964, 426). Though contemporary stylistics has much to say about how one describes that *way*,[1] Anglo-Saxon scholars face the more difficult problem of discovering the way the ancient scops did *it*.

Until very recently, critical comment about style in Old English poetry has fitted neatly into one traditional category or

Complete bibliographical information for all works referred to by author and date is provided in the list of "Works Cited" at the end of the essay.

1. See, for example, Donald C. Freeman, ed., *Linguistics and Literary Style* (New York 1970); Seymour Chatman, ed., *Literary Style: A Symposium* (London and New York 1971); and idem, *Approaches to Poetics* (New York 1973).

1

another. Ohmann provides a convenient list of these classifications: national or period styles, sound, tropes, imagery, attitude, structure, particular and local effects, special idiosyncrasies, lexical and grammatical features (423–25). And, in common practice, the study of Old English poetic style has also embraced origin, genre, meaning, and value. The lines between these divisions are hard to draw, and no two writers on style have precisely the same focus. This essay will treat only general considerations, based on the actual commentary on style in Old English poetry. The highly technical and the overly speculative will not be represented: Old English metrics would furnish many curiosities, but that would also require a separate investigation.[2]

No subject entirely escapes its history, and one fact in the discipline of Anglo-Saxon shines more brightly (or more dimly) than any other: from the start the surviving texts have been studied mainly for extra-literary concerns. English anti-Papists read and exploited Anglo-Saxon prose in their political and theological battles for a hundred years before any edition of Anglo-Saxon poetry appeared.[3] Junius first presented a significant body of that poetry (the Caedmon poems, 1655), but with small regard for literary qualities; he notes only that the contents of his manuscript correspond to part of the works ascribed to Caedmon by Bede.[4] Milton's curt and unsympathetic comments on *The Battle of Brunanburh* aside,[5] Anglo-Saxon poetry received its initial description from George Hickes in his *Thesaurus* (1705). Most of Hickes's more preposterous ideas were dismissed by the time of the early nineteenth

NB

NB

2. For a brief overview of the history of this subject, see R. W. Burchfield, "The Prosodic Terminology of Anglo-Saxon Scholars," in *Old English Studies in Honour of John C. Pope*, ed. Robert B. Burlin and Edward B. Irving, Jr. (Toronto 1974) 171–202.

3. See Eleanor N. Adams, *Old English Scholarship in England from 1566–1800* (New Haven, 1917) 11–84; and John Petheram, *An Historical Sketch of the Progress and Present State of Anglo-Saxon Literature in England* (London 1840) passim.

4. Quoted in Benjamin Thorpe, ed., *Caedmon's Metrical Paraphrase of Parts of the Holy Scriptures, in Anglo-Saxon* (London 1832) xvii.

5. See Robinson's essay below at n. 3.

century; John Kemble called the *Thesaurus* "that miracle of ill directed industry and mistaken learning" (Kemble 1837, 12). But Hickes stands at the head of a long line of scholars who, while devoted to the study of northern antiquity, were puzzled, startled, and even horrified by the barbarity they found. Their conviction that Anglo-Saxon poetry represented the art of an infant race provided a handy means of excusing crudity: the poems were barbaric, so they thought, because they had no recognizable rhythmic or prosodic standard, and lacked similes and other classical rhetorical embellishments. Hickes based a more specific apology on his odd opinions concerning the history of Anglo-Saxon dialects. Old English he divided into three periods: British (or pure) Saxon, Dano-Saxon, and Norman- (or Semi-) Saxon. To explain the many obscurities and problems connected with reading Old English, he turns against the Danes, a coarse people who tainted the pristine Saxon tongue. I quote from *Wotton's Short View of George Hickes's . . . Archeological Treasure of the Ancient Northern Languages*:

> This Dialect differs from the purer *Saxon*, which King Ælfred, Ælfric, Lupus, and others used, as well in the Words, which are most of them either *Cimbric* or *Teutonic*, as in the Orthography, and the almost general Disregard to Grammatical Rules, being the Product of the *Danes* and *Normans*; who, as a rude and an illiterate People in all Respects, and for the most part Pirates, corrupted the Anglo-Saxon Language (*Wotton* 1735, 11).

Only *Caedmon's Hymn* survives as a poetic remnant of the original dialect. For Hickes, Anglo-Saxon was difficult and *spinosa*, "thorny" (Hickes 1705, 177).[6] Although he assures his reader that the study of Anglo-Saxon poetry will be both "pleasant and useful," *jucunda ac utilia* (203), he still feels pressed to offer a series of rules to assist the uninitiated (who may be able to read some Old English prose) in picking his

6. All translations from Latin are my own, unless a specific reference is given; translations from German are based on the notes of my research assistant, Harriet Woolf.

way through the sharp spines of Old English verse. He warns
the hardy to beware of the obscure transpositions of words, the
cryptic periphrases and tropes, the syntactic violations (especially asyndetic constructions), the frequency of synonymic
appositions, and the elliptic phrases (198–203). But of one
thing he is quite sure: the rules of Old English prosody are
clear and uniform and could be perceived if we had sufficient
knowledge of their syllabication.[7] Hickes's laborious attempt
to square Old English metrics with the quantitative verse of
Greek and Latin poetry was an enterprise doomed to failure,
although the establishing of prosodic rules occupied most of
his and other early commentators' time. Later scholars quickly
dispensed with Hickes's whimsical solutions.

Eleanor Adams writes, somewhat inaccurately, of Hickes:
he "recognizes that the Old English poetry lacks end-rhyme,
but seems unaware of its peculiar alliterative quality" (Adams
1917, 89). First, Hickes did perceive that rhyme occured—if
rarely—in the poetry (198); second, he also noticed what he
calls the "harmony" or "consonance" of initial letters, what
we refer to as alliteration (Hickes 1711, 40). However, he failed
to see alliteration as the structural principle of the Old English
verse line. Instead he argues that alliteration comes from the
Muses and can be found "in all the poems of all peoples," *in
omnibus omnium gentium poëmatis initialium illa consonantia
auditur* (Hickes 1705, 195), and he provides examples in
Greek, Latin, Old Icelandic, and Middle and Modern English
to prove his claim (Hickes 1705, 195–97). Hickes's confusion
on the alliterative principle clouded discussions of Anglo-
Saxon prosody for over a century; not until Conybeare (1813)
and Rask (1817) did clarity begin to emerge.

The eighteenth century lagged far behind the seventeenth in
the pursuit of Anglo-Saxon studies (Adams 1917, 85–113).

7. Again, Wotton gives a concise summary of Hickes's position:
First, They strictly observed Metre or the Quantity of Feet; I mean
short and long Syllables, varied by a certain Rule. This is to us the
more obscure because we are ignorant of the just Quantities of all
their Syllables. Their Verses were for the most Part of four, five, or six
Syllables (Wotton 1735, 17–18).

Comments on Old English poetic style are rare, and those we do chance upon always fit into some other scheme. Anglo-Saxon poetry is not a main subject.

Johnson's well-known essay on the history of the English language contains little on Anglo-Saxon literature. The language itself, he writes, "having been always cursory and extemporaneous, must have been artless and unconnected, without any modes of transition or involution of clauses; which abruptness and inconnection may be observed even in their later writings" (Johnson 1755, D¹). On poetry itself, Johnson faintly echoes Hickes:

> Of the *Saxon* poetry some specimen is necessary, though our ignorance of the laws of their metre and the quantities of their syllables, which it would be very difficult, perhaps impossible, to recover, excludes us from that pleasure which the old bards undoubtedly gave to their contemporaries.
>
> The first poetry of the *Saxons* was without rhyme, and consequently must have depended upon the quantity of their syllables; but they began in time to imitate their neighbours, and close their verses with correspondent sounds (E¹).

Even these brief remarks let us see how Johnson shared the neoclassical prejudices against barbaric art.

 Bishop Percy affords an excellent example of a learned and perceptive literary scholar, who has all the information he needs to come to the proper conclusions, but who cannot grasp the whole truth. Percy's Icelandic studies made him well acquainted with the principles of alliteration in Scandinavian poetry, which he illustrates at some length. Percy derives his knowledge of Norse literature from Wormius, whom he finds in Hickes's *Thesaurus*; but he does not make the imaginative leap which would have permitted him to establish a parallel with Anglo-Saxon poetry. These are his observations set down in his essay "On the Metre of Pierce Plowman's Visions":

> Their brethren the Anglo-Saxon poets occasionally used the same kind of alliteration, and it is common to meet in their writings with similar examples of the foregoing rules. Take an instance or two in modern characters:

> "*Sk*eop tha and *Sk*yrede   "*H*am and *H*eahsetl
> *Sk*yppend ure."   *H*eofena rikes."
>
> I know not however that there is any where extant an intire
> Saxon poem all in this measure. But distichs of this sort perpe-
> tually occur in all their poems of any length.
>
> Now, if we examine the versification of *Pierce Plowman's
> Visions*, we shall find it constructed exactly by these rules (Per-
> cy 1765, 261).

From our perspective, it is easy to condescend. Yet the failure
to see the importance of alliteration was so common in the
eighteenth century that we should not single out Bishop Percy
for special censure.

The four editions of Thomas Warton's *History of English
Poetry* (1774; 1824, edited by Richard Price; 1840, edited by
Richard Taylor; 1871, edited by W. C. Hazlitt) offer a chronicle in miniature of Old English scholarship during the century
they span. We move from Warton's cavalier and predictable
commentary in 1774 to Henry Sweet's full chapter, commis-
sioned especially for the 1871 edition. In the first edition Warton justifies his dismissal of the whole corpus of "Saxon
poetry" thus: "Our Saxon poems are for the most part little
more than religious rhapsodies. . . . The principal products of
the most eminent monasteries for three centuries were incredi-
ble legends which discovered no marks of invention, unedify-
ing homilies, and trite exposition of the scriptures," (Warton
1774, vi and n.p.). By 1824, the date of the second edition of
Warton's *History*, a significant change takes place: Richard
Price composes a lengthy "Editor's Preface" for Warton's
work, and he comments: "Indeed there is nothing more striking, or more interesting to the ardent philologer, than the
order and regularity preserved in Anglo-Saxon composition,
the variety of expression, the innate richness, and plastic
power with which the language is endowed" (Price 1824, 112).

Late in the eighteenth century some of Hickes's misconcep-
tions came under attack, though not, unfortunately, without
replacement by others equally erroneous. Thomas Tyrwhitt,
best known for his edition of *The Canterbury Tales*, challenges
Hickes's theories of quantitative meter. In "An Essay on the

Language and Versification of Chaucer," he lists Hickes's reasons for supposing quantity to be the basis of that meter and then concludes with a rather astonishing proposition of his own:

> However specious these reasons may appear, they are certainly far from conclusive. . . . For my own part, I confess myself unable to discover any material distinction of the Saxon Poetry from Prose, except a greater pomp of diction, and a more stately kind of march. Our ancestors affected a certain pomp of style in all their compositions. . . . And this affectation, I suspect, was the true cause of their so frequently inverting the natural order of their words, especially in Poetry. The obscurity arising from these inversions had the appearance of Pomp. That they were not owing to the constraint of any metrical Laws (as Hickes supposes) may be presumed from their being commonly used in Prose, and even in Latin Prose by Saxon writers. . . . We do not see any marks of studied alliteration in the old Saxon Poetry; so that we might attribute the introduction of that practice to the Danes, if we were certain, that it made a part of the Scaldic versification at the time of the Danish settlements in England (Tyrwhitt 1775, 47–49).

John Josias Conybeare was later to make an elaborate apology for these notions (Conybeare 1826, vi–vii).

All these misinformed opinions come from men not primarily, if at all, interested in Anglo-Saxon peotry. One can readily forgive Tyrwhitt and the others because this period in literary history lay outside their special interests; one has less tolerance when Sharon Turner, the major Anglo-Saxon scholar of his day, delivers similar, and even more perverse, sentiments. Writing in 1840, John Petheram gives this summation of Turner's effect on Anglo-Saxon studies:

> The publication of the first edition of Sharon Turner's History of the Anglo-Saxons in successive volumes between the years 1799 and 1805, appears to have excited an attention not only towards their history, but by the addition to it of an account of their language and literature, a slow but gradually increasing attention has been awakened; a deep, and, from time to time, a still deeper interest has been created amongst us, as one after

another of the literary productions of our simple and unpre-
tending ancestors have been brought into view from their sleep
of ages, till at last we forget the dim glimmerings of light which
appeared in the sixteenth century in the effulgence which now
surrounds our path (Petheram 1840, 118).

This is Romantic Gothicism tuned to a mystical experience.
And when we look at Turner, we can only wonder how his negative pronouncements on the style of Old English poetry produced Petheram's enthusiastic response. One substantial quotation from Turner's *History* reveals all his prejudices, some of
which can be traced back to Hickes and projected forward
even to the present:[8]

> In the Anglo-Saxon poetry [figures] took the peculiar shape of
> the metaphor and the periphrasis. The imagination exerted
> itself in framing those abrupt and imperfect links or fragments
> of similes which we call metaphors: and the feeling expressed
> its emotions by that redundant repetition of phrases, which,
> though it added little to the meaning of the poet's lay, was yet
> the emphatic effusion of his heart, and excited consenting
> sympathies in those to whom it was addressed. This habit of
> paraphrasing the sentiment is the great peculiarity of the mind
> of the Anglo-Saxon peotry; the metaphor may be frequently
> observed, but the periphrasis is never long absent.
>   The style of their poetry was as peculiar. It has been much
> disputed by what rules or laws the Saxons arranged their poet-
> ical phrases. I have observed a passage in the general works of

8. See, for example, the comments on style in Old English poetry by
James E. Cross: "At a first reading Old English poetry appears prolix and
cumbersome . . . yet also strange and exciting. The excitement is caused by
the prevalence of poetic alternatives. . . . There were also equivalents in
compound words or phrases which were originally metaphors or condensed
similes, e.g. *beaduleoma*. . . . When used thoughtfully, these stylistic features can produce a tightly-made yet richly-suggestive and subtle poetry, but
even here a caveat must be given that these features, indeed the very words
or phrases, are used so often by poets that they can lose their pictorial or
descriptive content and become merely alternative words for the object. . . .
[Variation] leads to prolixity of expression, sometimes poor expression, when
the word or phrase calls up another by reflex action of the memory without
regard to presentation of thought." "The Old English Period," in *History of
Literature in the English Language*, Vol. 1: *The Middle Ages*, ed. Whitney
F. Bolton (London 1970) 12–66 at 17–18.

Bede which may end the controversy, by showing that they used no rules at all, but adopted the simpler principle of consulting only the natural love of melody (Turner 1828, 264).

Beyond this, the style of Saxon poetry is (again) "barbarous," "barren," "artificial," "common," "imperfect," and "half-formed" (270–71). Even in the fifth edition of his *History*, which appeared long after the work of Conybeare, Rask, and Bosworth, he has not renounced the old eighteenth-century error concerning alliteration. Turner concedes only a small portion of ground: "I am willing to concur with Mr. J. Conybeare, that alliteration was used in Saxon poetry. The examples in his introductory essay show it . . ., but I think it was as an occasional beauty, not as in Pierce Ploughman, the fundamental principle" (357–58, n. 4).

A decade before Conybeare, George Ellis repeats Tyrwhitt's views on quantity and alliteration and joins Turner in an estimation of Anglo-Saxon poetic style:

> The variety of inflection, by which the Anglo-Saxon language was distinguished from the modern English, gave to their poets an almost unlimited power of inversion; and they used it almost without reserve: not so much perhaps for the purpose of varying the cadence of their verse, as with a view to keep the attention of their hearers upon the stretch, by the artificial obscurity of their style; and to astonish them by those abrupt transitions which are very commonly (though rather absurdly) considered as Pindaric, and which are the universal characteristic of savage poetry (Ellis 1801, 12–13).

These opinions, very much in vogue, disappeared slowly.

After Turner and Ellis at the beginning of the century, three scholars dominate the study of Old English poetic style—John Josias Conybeare, Rasmus Rask, and Joseph Bosworth. In different ways each moved the study of Old English forward, though they all held on to many of the biases of their predecessors. Conybeare and Bosworth subscribe to an evolutionary view of poetry, present from the beginning and emphasized by Turner. Approving generously of Turner's remarks on Anglo-Saxon poetry, Conybeare writes:

That gentleman has particularly noticed the constant accumulation of equivalent, or nearly equivalent, words and phrases,
which, as it generally constitutes the chief and earliest orna-
ment of the poetry of rude and illiterate nations, appears in
that of our Saxon ancestors to have supplied almost entirely
the place of those higher graces and resources of composition,
which are the natural results of a more advanced state of civil
society. (Conybeare 1826, xxviii)

Bosworth pays Turner even greater respect and takes over
his general comments on the poetry "almost verbatim" (Bosworth 1823, xxxii and 209–12). Not until nearly twenty years
later did a scholar speak plainly about Turner's *History*. John
Kemble finds it "a learned and laborious work; yet in all that
relates to the language and the poetry of our forefathers, often
deficient, often mistaken. It is painful to be compelled to
speak in terms like these of a work which in many respects
deserves great praise" (Kemble 1837, 25). Rasmus Rask's de-
valuation of Old English poems has less to do with ideas of historical progress than with national pride; he measures the
poetical monuments of the Anglo-Saxon against those in Icelandic and finds the former seriously wanting:

The Anglo-Saxon Language, as well as its literature, holds un-
questionably a rank inferior to the ancient Scandinavian, in
respect both of intrinsic excellence, and of interest and importance. . . . We find for the most part, Translations from the
Latin, Chronicles, Homilies, and Treatises upon subjects
which, in the present times, are but of little value. Nor, when
considered with regard to style, do these works possess any
great claim to attention, as they seem, almost without exception, deficient, both in taste, and peculiarity of character
(Rask 1830, iii–iv).

Bosworth integrates conflicting opinions by setting out in pre-
cise categories the main features of Anglo-Saxon poetry.
Under the section entitled "Prosody" we find subsections on
"Alliteration," "Emphasis," "Rhythm," "Rime," "Inversion
and Transition," "The Omission of Particles," "Their Short
Phrases," "Periphrasis," "Metaphors," and "Parallelism,"—

that is, all the poetic features which had troubled scholars with more refined tastes (Bosworth 1823, 212–36). While Bosworth's work remains completely unoriginal, he does provide the first schema of poetic devices drawn from the scattered comments made for over a century.

In his discussion of "Parallelism" Bosworth carefully notes that the credit for identifying this aspect belongs to Conybeare, whose clerical background gave him a wide acquaintance with Hebraic poetry. In the "Second Communication on the Metre of Anglo-Saxon Poetry," read before the Society of Antiquaries on Dec. 9, 1813, Conybeare claims

> There is, however, one peculiarity of construction occurring in the poetical remains of the Anglo-Saxons, which, as far as my knowledge extends, has not been mentioned by any preceding writer; and which, nevertheless, is so generally prevalent in them, as to preclude, I think, all supposition of its being other than the effect of design. I mean an artificial arrangement of the several phrases or clauses of which the sentence is constituted, in a manner somewhat resembling . . . the sacred poetry of the Hebrews, and termed . . . *Parallelism* (Conybeare 1826, xxviii–xxix).

Conybeare recognizes the feature and rests satisfied with marking out the particulars. Perhaps because *Parallelism* had the sanction of Biblical verse, it escaped censure in Anglo-Saxon. But Conybeare's acceptance of a native "design" for Old English poetry lays the foundation for later work dealing with the style and esthetics of that corpus on its own terms and not as a deviation from classical standards.

Whether Conybeare or Rask was the first to establish alliteration as the ruling principle for Old English poetry is moot. A good portion of Conybeare's "First Communication," read in February of 1813, discusses alliteration; the "Second Communication" takes alliteration as its principal subject. Although Conybeare disclaims from the start that "little perhaps can be added to the observations of the laborious Hickes" (xxvii), his own lecture proves the contrary. His essay does not cover the full range of rules governing alliteration, though it provides an intelligent beginning:

> Our ancestors do not appear to have been anxious to construct
> their alliterative systems with the intricacy or variety said to be
> discoverable in those of the northern Scalds; . . . they were
> more partial to the recurrence of consonants than vowels; and
> . . . they were usually studious of throwing the alliteration on
> the emphatic syllables. I do not recollect any instance of an
> attempt to carry on the same alliteration through a consider-
> able number of lines together (xxvii–xxviii).

Originally read in 1813, published the next year in *Archaeo-
logia*, and reprinted by his brother William in 1826, these
remarks on alliteration overlap Rask's pronouncement which
first appeared in Danish (1817) and was then translated into
English by Thorpe (1830). Presumably William Conybeare
knew of Rask's work, for the notes and "Addenda" make his
brother's words much more schematic (xvii–xxxvi).

Rask everywhere speaks slightingly of English scholars and
implicitly scolds them for not having discovered these basic
laws:

> The Anglo-Saxon versification, like the Icelandic, and that of
> the other ancient Gothic nations, has a peculiar construction,
> the chief characteristic of which does not, as in the Phrygian
> tongues, consist in syllabic quantity, but in *Alliterative Rime*,
> or *Alliteration*; that is, when, in two immediately successive,
> and connected, lines, there occur three words, beginning with
> the same letter, and so that the third, or last, word stands first
> in the second line, and the two others in the first line: the ini-
> tial letters, in these three words, are then called *riming letters*.
> The last of these letters is considered as the *chief letter*; after
> which the two letters, in the preceding verse, which are called
> *sub-letters*, must be adjusted (Rask 1830, 135).

Rask's long series of rules required revision, as Edwin Guest
indignantly demonstrated. Rask, he says, only applied "the
rules which Olaus Wormius laid down for the regulation of
Scandinavian verse"[9] to the recalcitrant Anglo-Saxon. This is

---

9. Guest's work must be seen in context. Besides his nationalistic prejudice, Guest's attack on Rask stems from his acceptance of respected opinions.

Samuel Fox's remarks on alliteration, written in 1830, well after Rask and
Conybeare, illustrate the confusion of the times: "in many instances, as is

a serious objection (Guest 1838, 141); yet Rask seems to have assigned alliteration its proper place. And even Rask was not entirely irascible; his second edition contains an acknowledgement that "Mr. Conybeare has the merit of being the first that noticed this kind of verse," that is, the hypermetric or long lines in what he took to be Caedmon (Rask 1830, 163 and Bosworth 1823, 244–47).

NB

In the next few decades of the nineteenth century, the most active scholars were more concerned with historical, archeological and editorial problems than with esthetic issues. Under the influence of Jakob Grimm, John Kemble and others were at work reconstructing that Romantic ideal of the Teutonic past which E. G. Stanley has recently dismantled.[10] One or two transformations manifest themselves: a shift in taste occurs permitting appreciation of some qualities previously denigrated, and this leads to a more favorable impression of the poetry. The source for this new estimate reflects changed attitudes towards the language itself, which Thorpe finds had "the strength of iron, with the sparkling and the beauty of burnished steel" (Thorpe 1868, v). The natural strength of the language makes Kemble prize the absence of similes:

> Similes were originally unknown, being replaced by metaphors: . . . in the Vercelli poems there are several, and one or two which have a smack of abstraction about them strongly indicative of an advanced (and corrupt) state of civilization. A fresh and lively nature, which does not analyse the processes of thought, but trusts itself and its own feeling, can venture, for example, to call a ship a "sea-bird" without checking itself, and saying that "it goes along *like* a sea-bird" (Kemble 1843, ix).

---

seen in the [*Menologium*], the alliteration is obscure, and in others, altogether undiscoverable. It is impossible at the present day to ascertain, whether alliteration was an essential to poetry among the Saxon bards, or not; because, although it is not unfrequently absent, this proves nothing, as it might arise from officious ignorance in those who were entrusted to transcribe the existing MSS" (Samuel Fox, ed., *Menologium seu Calendarium Poeticum* [London 1830] v–vi).

10. See E. G. Stanley, *The Search for Anglo-Saxon Paganism* (Cambridge 1975; reprint of articles in *Notes and Queries* 209–210 [1964/5]).

Kemble's Rousseauistic enthusiasms did not influence later critics who held the lack of similes in Old English poetry one of its major flaws.

The general change seems most marked in the words of Thomas Wright. He still subscribes to Turner's esthetic commentary, but replaces his strictures with a genuine appreciation:

> The Anglo-Saxon poetry has come down to us in its own native dress. In unskilful hands it sometimes became little more than alliterative prose; but, as far as it is yet known to us, it never admitted any adventitious ornaments. Having been formed in a simple state of society, it admits, by its character, no great variety of style, but generally marches on in one continued strain of pomp and grandeur, to which the Anglo-Saxon language itself was in its perfect state peculiarly suited. The principal characteristic of this poetry is an endless variety of epithet and metaphor, which are in general very expressive, although their beauty sometimes depends so much on the feelings and manners of the people for whom they were made, that they appear to us rather fanciful. As, however, these poets drew their pictures from nature, the manner in which they apply their epithets, like the rich colouring of the painter, produces a brilliant and powerful impression on the mind (Wright 1842, 8-9).[11]

Early editions of Anglo-Saxon poetry did not concern themselves with matters of style. John Kemble's few remarks made in his *editio princeps* of the *Vercelli MS* hold true for Thorpe's *Caedmon* (1832) and the same editor's *The Exeter Book* (1842), and for Jakob Grimm's *Andreas and Elene* (1840). Grimm deals briefly with the typical use of certain formulaic phrases in the poetry, though he does not, of course, use that term, and he also lists some of the recurrent metaphors found in Old English poetic diction. As always, he underlines the tension inherent in the application of a heathen Germanic diction to foreign subject matter—here, the hagiographical legends of Mediterranean Christianity (Grimm 1840, xxxii–xlvii).

The long dispute over the authorship of the Caedmon

11. See also Henry Wadsworth Longfellow's somewhat less rapturous essay, "Anglo-Saxon Literature," *North American Review* 47 (1839) 90-134.

poems, like the later debate over the Cynewulf canon, created a critical methodology to answer the following question (a query raised again in a new form by the oral formulaicists after 1953): which aspects of Anglo-Saxon poetic style are part of the tradition and which belong solely to the scop who wrote (or sang) the poem? Junius thought Caedmon composed all the poems in the manuscript now identified informally as the Caedmon manuscript, but he used only external evidence from Bede to reach this conclusion. Hickes denies they were by Caedmon; but in attributing them to some barbaric Dano-Saxon, he still imagines their having a single author. Conybeare finds Hickes's contentions unconvincing (Conybeare 1826, 185), and Thorpe writes, "I see no good foundation for doubt upon the subject; and . . . I feel inclined to regard the work as the production of the good Monk of Whitby" (Thorpe 1832, viii). Only Conybeare, however, reveals any sensitivity to the conspicuous differences in style among the five poems. He catches the disparities between what we now call *Genesis A* and *Genesis B*, the latter having a style so different from the "meagre style" of the former, that "it seems to have formed originally a distinct composition" (Conybeare 1826, 188). With the return to the *Exodus*, Conybeare feels "the style again becomes more spirited" (189).

Given this background, it is all the more remarkable to come upon Ernst Götzinger's dissertation on Caedmon (1860). He concludes that *Genesis*, *Exodus* and *Daniel* are notably different from one another. *Exodus* contains the best poetry; *Genesis* and *Daniel* are lesser works of equal value. If each poem were the work of one author, we would expect them to bear the same poetic mark, and, since this is not the case, we must assume different authors for each (Götzinger 1860, 34). Götzinger's procedures now seem naive and rudimentary. Although he treats questions of phonology, he relies mainly on lexical distinctions, a base too small (and too little explored in that time) on which to erect a larger hypothesis concerning authorship. So Heinrich Ziegler criticizes Götzinger and also Balg[12] for limiting themselves to the lexicon in their studies of

12. See Hugo Balg, *Der Dichter Cædmon und seine Werke* (Bonn 1882).

Caedmon's works, and not taking the whole sphere of stylistics into account (Ziegler 1883, 1). Götzinger's methods may be easy to fault, but this should not obscure his importance in seeing fundamental stylistic differences among poems formerly assumed to share a common author and style.

The lone French writer of importance on Anglo-Saxon style in the nineteenth century is Hippolyte Taine. Much of what he says in his *History of English Literature* (1864) comes out of a long, and now recognizable, line of commentary. He is one of the most extreme of such critics:

> If there has ever been anywhere a deep and serious poetic sentiment, it is here. They do not speak, they sing, or rather they shout. Each little verse is an acclamation, which breaks forth like a growl; their strong breasts heave with a groan of anger or enthusiasm, and a vehement or indistinct phrase or expression rises suddenly, almost in spite of them, to their lips. . . . The fifty rays of light which every phenomenon emits in succession to a regular and well-directed intellect, come to them at once in a glowing and confused mass. . . . Here all is imagery. . . . But whatever be the imagery, here as in Iceland, though unique, it is too feeble. . . . [the poet's] ideas are entangled without order; without notice, abruptly, the poet will return to the idea he has quitted, and insert it in the thought to which he is giving expression. It is impossible to translate these incongruous ideas, which quite disconcert our modern style. At times they are unintelligible. Articles, particles, everything capable of illuminating thought, of marking the connection of terms, of producing regularity of ideas, all rational and logical artifices, are neglected. . . . It is the acme of barbarism (Taine 1873, 45–47).

Such a broadside can only come from someone who knows for certain what poetry is before he reads any new poem. Taine shares this assurance with all his contemporaries—British, German, or American.

Richard Heinzel (1875) first treated systematically some major features of Old English poetic style; yet he, too, had fixed preconceptions. Trained in the burgeoning school of comparative Indo-European philology, Heinzel applies its methods and assumptions to the study of style. He begins with the premise that all techniques used in Germanic epic texts are older than the epics themselves, being derived from earlier hymnic poetry (Heinzel 1875, 16). In addition, he maintains that whatever is found in older Indo-European literatures must have been present at some stage in all the branches of Germanic poetry. The simile, for example, is one of the most refined of poetic devices. Similes occur in the Vedas, in Homer, and in Old Norse poetry, but rarely appear in any branch of West Germanic literature; thus West Germanic style is decadent and represents a decline from previous Indo-European achievements (17). Francis Gummere (1881) finds the weakness in this part of Heinzel's thesis without difficulty: the evidence Heinzel presents can be interpreted in another way, for the simile may well have developed independently in each language and not have been an original part of the repertoire of Indo-European poetic effects (Gummere 1881, 5).

By classifying in detail the shared characteristics of *altgermanische* poetry, Heinzel makes the esthetic of this "rude" poetry legitimate. Variation,[13] parallelism, the "preposed" pronoun, and the separation of explanatory or decorative appositions from the word to which they refer he explores fully. Heinzel sees an order in the disjointed succession of ideas which had troubled, indeed infuriated, so many of his predecessors. The Anglo-Saxons had a special fondness for an ABA sequential pattern, and this he compares to the metrical technique he calls "crossed alliteration" (3–12). More sophisticated analysis will eventually call this feature "interlace"; however, Heinzel deserves credit for having seen the alternation as deliberate and valid rather than accidental and inept. His analogy between narrative sequence and metrical device is also the first endeavor to relate the poetry's micro-techniques to macro-structures; Tolkien later tried to do much the same, with similarly limited success, when he related the balanced antithesis in the overall structure of *Beowulf* to the antithesis inherent in the Anglo-Saxon line (Tolkien 1936, 271–73). Most importantly Heinzel apprehends that such deviations

13. On Heinzel as the inventor of the term "variation," see Robinson's essay below at n. 6.

from the "natural" order of thoughts and words can only be partially explained by freedom in word order. Greek and Latin enjoy even greater syntactic flexibility and yet they do not reveal the lack of "sequentiality" found in Anglo-Saxon poetry. Heinzel attributes this propensity for "entangled" order, not to Anglo-Saxon grammar, but to the Anglo-Saxon mind, which preferred to think of several things simultaneously, instead of working out each separate idea in logical stages. Taine also recognized this bent, and he did not like it; Tolkien refers to the same phenomenon when he speaks of *Beowulf*'s "*static* structure" (272).

Heinzel's treatment of style becomes less impressive when he turns from description of textual features to subjective reactions and esthetic remarks. Kennings predominate in Old Norse literature, he believes, since that society placed strong emphasis on "sensuous vividness" (Heinzel 1875, 20). In Old English he finds the reverse, a tendency toward intellectualization, although (somewhat paradoxically) Old English poetry stands apart from other Germanic literatures *because* of its highly emotional aspect (23 and 30–31). The sentimentality which Heinzel discovers in the Old English epics he ascribes to the obtrusive influence of Christianity (38). Heinzel's biases rise to the surface in his treatment of Cynewulf, a poet whose descriptions, he writes, always hover above the objects, and who omits details essential to the narration. But given Cynewulf's "melting softness," his idealistic orientation which trembles before earthly things, such traits may be excused (43f.).

In his reply to Heinzel, Gummere restricts himself to the simile and the metaphor; still some of his own spiritual and racial preferences vitiate the rejoinder. Gummere's reasoning is circular: the absence of simile in Old English poetry follows from "the passionate nature of the Germanic race [which] is thoroughly opposed to the use and development of the simile" (10). Next Gummere takes issue with Heinzel on the question of the "softness" of Old English poetry. He maintains this has nothing to do with Christianity; it is only another manifestation of "a tendency to melancholy that extends throughout English literature generally" (10). Finally, Gummere believes we should not lament the deficiency of simile when Old English poetry has an abundance of metaphor, the "cornerstone of all poetical style" (11).

By Gummere's account, the origin of metaphor is "A confusion, or if one will, flexibility of terms" (11). Metaphors are the poetic techniques of a race in its childhood. On the nature and typology of metaphor, Gummere writes:

> Such is the general nature of the A. S. metaphor. There is a gap between concrete and abstract, but it is narrow, and the poet leaps from one to the other without any sense of inconsistency. . . . The typical A. S. metaphor was originally confined to one word, or at the furthest, to several words that stood in the closest syntactical relation. This general type has been invaded by the influence of the Latin literature of the church, especially by the hymns; the result, whether as extended metaphor, simile, or learned allegory, is found not as much in Beowulf as in the Caedmon poems, but even here to no overwhelming degree.
>
> In short, a decidedly foreign influence, but no so great as materially to detract from the originality of the native style (16, 53).

Gummere's definition of metaphor does not measure up to modern conceptions,[14] but his treatise was influential in its day and probably did more to inhibit further study than to promote it.

A. Hoffmann's rebuttal (1883) of both Heinzel and Gummere starts with a pertinent question: if Germanic passion prevented the development of the simile in Old English, why did it flourish in Old Norse (A. Hoffmann 1883, 164–65)? He sets out to determine which aspects of Norse style created favorable conditions for similes, and which qualities in Anglo-Saxon acted as restraints. The execution of his comparative plan falls far short of his aims. He relies again and again on his impressions of the two literatures to provide "reasons" for the difference: an interesting example of nineteenth-century

14. See, for example, I. A. Richards, *The Philosophy of Rhetoric* (London and New York 1936); Terence Hawkes, *Metaphor* (London 1972); Philip E. Wheelwright, *Metaphor and Reality* (Bloomington Ind. 1962); and Warren A. Shibles, comp., *Essays on Metaphor* (Whitewater Wisc. 1972).

"inductive" stylistics, with results little better than those of the neoclassicists. Hoffmann offers this summation: the descriptive techniques in the Edda draw mainly on fantasy, while in *Beowulf* they depend more on feeling and compassion. And since imagery evolves from fantasy, the poet whose description rests on life-like vividness will naturally compose in a more imagistic style. The Edda and the Homeric poems therefore manifest a great density of images; these epics possess that sensuousness of description which is not present in Old English (190). For Hoffmann, the "proven" reflective quality of Old English poetry likewise restricts metonymy, and also explains the many Anglo-Saxon euphemisms (frequently noted in the nineteenth century) for death and dying, the relative lack of kennings, and the reluctance to use personification (192–93).

However unsound many of Hoffmann's premises may be, his significant contribution lies in perceiving that the style of much Old English poetry is rhetorical and abstract; it developed as a compensation for the loss of the rich store of images present in early hymnic poetry. But, he writes, the disappearance of imagery does not mean that Old English poetic style has decayed from a purer state. Such rhetorical figures as variation and antithesis have simply replaced images at the same time as they provided a deterrent to a resurgence of the earlier style.

Two important general studies appeared in 1883, Reinhold Merbot's *Ästhetische Studien zur angelsächsischen Poesie* and Heinrich Ziegler's *Der poetische Sprachgebrauch in den sogen. Caedmonschen Dichtungen*. Merbot views Heinzel's work as relevant to stylistic questions for all Germanic poetry, but of limited use for the idiosyncrasies of Anglo-Saxon style, which Merbot believes exist and can be described as discrete phenomena. Further, he posits a large body of common traits in the various manifestations of Old English style. For him, there is little distinction between the epic and lyric styles in Anglo-Saxon, some of the epics themselves preserving lyric elements derived from the primitive hymnic poetry (Merbot 1883, 31). He calls for a thorough rhetorical analysis of the topics and figures that characterize individual poems and a clarification of how single works relate to the whole, conventional style.

While Merbot does emphasize that the word-accumulations (*Worthäufigen*), repetitions, excessive elaboration, episodic structure and epic breadth of Old English poetry in no way correspond to any modern conception of style, like most of his forerunners and contemporaries he cannot resist the final derogatory remark. Taking issue with Köhler, who held that the early style of Anglo-Saxon poetry was very bare (Köhler 1870, 48–49), Merbot dismisses the evidence of the lists in *Widsith* and proffers the notion that the prototypical style was much like the poetry that has survived. A practical poetry, a craft but not an art, it had no need to follow the laws of poetic composition. It produced a style of "intolerable harshness, gaps, unacceptable qualities, and signs of poor taste" (Merbot 1883, 50). Clarity and taste are products of a civilized society which the Anglo-Saxons had not yet attained. An old and familiar argument once more fails to come to terms with the traits of Anglo-Saxon style.

Ziegler's study of the Caedmon poems uses many of the rhetorical techniques which Merbot felt should be applied in any analysis; stylistic studies cannot, he maintains, employ only lexical data. The now accepted assumption that the Germans were a passionate breed explains for him the excitement and unrest found in Old English poetry, along with its obscurity and leaps in expression. Ziegler makes an analogy between the style and an uneven race in which the runners are "ideas" and "expression." But the ellipses, compounding, and use of appositional synonyms are comfortable devices for quickly fixing the racing ideas (Ziegler 1883, 31). Despite this fanciful premise, Ziegler's practical criticism shows quite remarkable precision and restraint. He demonstrates that the typical parathetic compounding of words—mere juxtaposition without elements of juncture—corresponds to the paratactic sentence structure; a significant instance of parallelism between lexical formation and syntax. He treats apposition at some length and connects the frequent ellipses with the freedom permitted in positioning. On the "accumulative" quality of Anglo-Saxon style, he notes that synonyms can be used either as additions to the original concepts or in apposition. And when he comments on the difficulty of discerning whether words in series are synonymic variation or the addition of something new, he raises an issue that only recent critics have managed well.[15]

The full range of Ziegler's work covers parallelism, repetition, synecdoche, metonymy (or lack of it, due to the emotional side of the Anglo-Saxon character), euphemism, and personification (63–128). His conclusions seem less important in the discussion of syntactic and tropic forms of discourse (154f.). According to Ziegler, the ordinary sentence in poetry is simple (as befits the excited Anglo-Saxon mode of thought), but unclear because of the many synonyms and repetitions. The final effect is an uneven mixture of movement and rest (150); and the absence of Homeric simile gives proof positive of an imaginative and intellectual weakness in Anglo-Saxon civilization (161–62).

In 1886 Wilhelm Bode undertook the first comprehensive investigation of the Anglo-Saxon kenning. His method and attitude characterize, indeed almost parody, the late nineteenth-century critics' passion for quantifying what they reluctantly tolerated. We learn, for example, that in all the Anglo-Saxon poetry known in Bode's time, which comprised 23,639 lines (excluding the Metrical Charms and the translations of the Psalms), there are 900 kennings for 54 different concepts. These occur 2,500 times, for an average of 1 kenning every 9 or 10 verses (Bode 1886, 11). He dismisses previous notions explaining the origin of this metaphor and substitutes an entirely mechanical alternative: kennings have not developed through the shift to epic from lyric or hymnic poetry, nor out of ancient Germanic passion, which must express a concept in every possible way, but rather from the alliterative verse form. Kennings and appositions only serve to fill out the second half-line and carry the alliteration; since kennings usually consist of two nouns with the first contributing little to the meaning,

15. See, for example, Stanley B. Greenfield, *The Interpretation of Old English Poems* (London 1972).

the presence of this initial word can be accounted for solely by the necessity of alliteration (13f.). Bode classified kennings into three different systems—their stylistic functions (descriptive, fixing in time and space, descriptive through comparison, etc.), their position in the chronology of Old English poetry (pre-Cynewulf, Cynewulf, and later), and their content (man, society, war, sea, etc.) (18f.). Later studies have superseded his effort, but in the late nineteenth century Bode's contemporaries prized it. So his opening remarks seem all the more puzzling:

> People with a serious and thorough rational education attempt, as a rule, to achieve a simple style, a direct means of expression. . . . When given the opportunity, the uneducated and half-educated favor the rich and ornamental style, which expresses thoughts as much as possible in an indirect manner, in conventional forms and half-understood phrases, in proverbs and high-sounding quotations. Kennings fit very well into this style; they are indirect and usually conventional, formulaic designations (9).

At base Bode's work is philological; he directs his attention to individual words and their metaphoric combinations. Much other stylistic criticism rests on a similar philological foundation. To be sure, the German universities produced hundreds of school programs and dissertations which examined the syntax and morphology of Old English poetic texts, but they were either grammatical in their focus, or they used style for dating and attribution. However, many scholars held to Hermann Gaebler's dictum (1880) that the best way to decide cases of authorship is to examine words and phrases, since no two poets ever have exactly the same vocabulary. To depend on syntax and morphology invites uncertainty, for these are influenced by the larger grammatical patterns of the language and dialect (Gaebler 1880, 503). Likewise Karl Schemann analyzes the synonyms in *Beowulf* to see if more than one poet had a hand in composing that poem. His premise is identical with Gaebler's: the same author will restrict himself to a relatively uniform diction; different authors will vary (Schemann 1882,

1-3). Schemann uses his data to disprove Müllenhoff's widely held view that *Beowulf* was a series of separate poems merely assembled in one manuscript by a later scribe (Müllenhoff 1869, 193-244). No one—except F. P. Magoun, and he from a rather different perspective[16]—now accepts Müllenhoff's theories, although Schemann's conclusions do not offer the soundest reasons for rejecting them (Schemann 1882, 99-101). The "disintegrators" had their day and passed on. Nevertheless in one or two cases they guessed accurately. Sievers's intuitive leap that led him to conclude the "interpolation" in *Genesis* was a translation of an Old Saxon text certainly proved true (Sievers 1875).

Gaebler, Schemann, and others insisted that diction should hold pride of place in the study of style. This emphasis raises the problem (yet once more) of the individual versus the formulaic in Anglo-Saxon vocabulary; or in late nineteenth-century academic terms, it recalls the famous quarrel between Sarrazin and Kail over *Parallelstellen* ("parallel passages").

Sarrazin issued what became a call to battle in an article on *The Fates of the Apostles*. He wished to prove by stylistic means that Cynewulf wrote *The Fates* and *Elene* at much the same time. He selects for this "objective statistical study of style" the nominal compounds in *The Fates*: these compounds are particularly characteristic of Anglo-Saxon style and especially significant for Cynewulf (Sarrazin 1889, 375-87). He relies on systematic listing and discovers many "parallels" between *The Fates* and Cynewulf's probable and certain works, especially *Elene*. On these grounds he assigns the poem, correctly it turns out, to Cynewulf.

Kail's retort is a barbed scholarly attack (Kail 1889, 21-40). He lists all the parallels between Cynewulf's poems and other Anglo-Saxon works and discovers so many instances of *Parallelstellen* that he can only conclude all of Anglo-Saxon poetry must have evolved under Cynewulf's influence (29-30). But

16. See Francis P. Magoun, Jr., *"Béowulf Á:* A Folk-Variant," *Arv* 14 (1958) 95-101; and *"Béowulf B:* A Folk-Poem on Béowulf's Death," in Arthur Brown and Peter Foote, eds., *Early English and Norse Studies, Presented to Hugh Smith in Honour of his Sixtieth Birthday* (London 1963) 127-40.

some poems do not share any parallel passages with Cynewulf, although they do exhibit parallels among themselves. Logically, then, one of two deductions follows: these passages must have been borrowed from lost Cynewulfian poems, or they must have arisen from other (also lost) models of epic style. There would then be no trace left of an independent Anglo-Saxon style, since such a style would have to be traced back to foreign influence (30). The absurdity of these propositions is obvious and Kail suggests instead that the *Parallelstellen* result from a common poetic repertory of formulae on which all Anglo-Saxon poets drew, quite independently of one another. The model of Anglo-Saxon diction and style must not be sought in any one poem, but reconstructed from the whole corpus of Anglo-Saxon poetry (32). Sarrazin's reply to Kail's criticism is not convincing (Sarrazin 1892, 186–92), for in fact Kail had hit on a truth about Anglo-Saxon poetry—its formulaic nature—that scholars are still trying to explore.

Not that the formulaic element had gone unnoticed; quite the contrary. With a few exceptions, everyone after Hickes makes note of the poetry's special and uniform diction. As early as 1885 O. Hoffmann had made a complete catalogue of Anglo-Saxon formulae, categorized by their syntactic composition (O. Hoffmann 1885, 48–88). A more comprehensive system appeared in 1889, the same year as the Sarrazin-Kail controversy. Richard Meyer proposed to collect all formulaic material in Old Germanic poetry and then to construct a whole poetic. His vague definition of the formula permits his realizing such a large undertaking; formulae are all means of expression which appear frequently enough to lend the poetry a particular character (Meyer 1889, 1). We need not pay inordinate attention to Meyer's abstract division of Germanic formulae into "symbolic" and "accentuating" (504f.). What does merit attention is his apt posing of the question: where do the individual poet and poem stand in relation to the range of the formulaic achievement of the people and the age (480)?

German scholars dominate the study of style in the last half of the nineteenth century. Whether involved in the compilation of lists or the creation of speculative theories, they did the spade work for all subsequent inquiry. The British, on the whole, seem uninterested in the matter; the Americans, under German influence, made one or two contributions, apart from Gummere's. Albert H. Tolman's article on "The Style of Anglo-Saxon Poetry" purports to be a full survey of the subject. Its range is broad, but Tolman finds a place for every cliché encountered in the history of stylistic criticism; it may stand as a distillation of the Victorian attitude (replete with prudishness) towards the style of Old English poetry (Tolman 1887, 17-47).

T. Gregory Foster succeeds somewhat better in isolating the exceptional stylistic features of *Judith*. His is not a novel approach; he still depends on lexical and grammatical analysis —the use of synonyms, compounds, sentence form, and figures of speech. *Judith*, he finds, resembles Cynewulfian poetry in many respects—in its terminology for God, its epithets for Holofernes, its wealth of kennings (Foster 1892, 70-73). On the other hand, the clarity of the narrative, the lack of parallel sentences and parenthetical expressions place *Judith* in a category different from any of the other Old English religious epics (85). Many typical devices have disappeared from this example of late Anglo-Saxon literature. In *Judith* the subordinate and co-ordinate clauses are "fittingly connected by conjunctions"; the "exaggerated accumulation of synonymous names" is gone; the poet has the decency to use pronouns so we can tell who is doing what, and pleonasm and the parallel sentence are entirely absent (86-87). Foster's study has most value for its description of what many critics designate as the last period in Anglo-Saxon style.

Literary histories furnish the richest store of a period's predispositions and esthetic concepts, and the late nineteenth century was the first great age of English literary history. Ten Brink's extraordinarily influential book (1877) contains two basic premises about the development of Germanic and Anglo-Saxon poetry: the ur-Germanic poems must have been hymnic and composed in strophes. Thus Anglo-Saxon style represents a considerable departure from the prototype (ten Brink 1889, 14). However, this development was arrested in Anglo-Saxon, with the result that the "epic movement in England did not reach its goal . . . [because of] the elements of poetic expression transmitted from the hymnic poetry" (17–18). He also believes that figures take root "in primitive-naïve and often mythical conception, [and] are so simple and obvious that, as in the language of every-day life, they are not felt to be figurative. Those turns of phrase, too, which impress us as decidedly metaphorical, are seldom very striking and hardly ever especially daring" (18). Ten Brink harbors most of the common prejudices against Anglo-Saxon poetry; he is in agreement with the Germanicists when he writes that "Christianity was doubtless one of the causes that destroyed the productive power of epic poetry . . ., the decay of the epic style . . . viz., the inclination to reflection, to elegiac tenderness" (28). He pays some close attention to differences among the poems, though his terms are impressionistic and judgmental at best: "poetic realism and sensuous coloring" "more animated," "prolix" (passim).

One of ten Brink's major contributions remains his general comments on Cynewulf, to whom for one reason or another practically all of Old English poetry had been assigned. Ten Brink sees "a conscious art" in Cynewulf's poetry. The imprint of Latin syntax and rhetoric in the poems is striking, even if Cynewulf's stylistic inheritance causes a predictable "diffuse treatment" of sources. As a Christian, Cynewulf writes necessarily in a more "subjective" style (55–56). Ten Brink's preferences come directly to the fore when he describes his favorite Anglo-Saxon poem:

> This song of *Byrhtnoth's Death* is one of the pearls of Old English poetry, full, as it is, of dramatic life, and of the fidelity of an eye-witness.[17] Its deep feeling throbs in the clear and powerful portrayal. In sharp contrast to the *Song of Brunanburh*, the lyrical element is still less prominent than in *Beowulf*. The style is simple, pithy, noble; compared with the epic, it is concise and even dry (96).

For him the objective, the masculine, the active, and the realistic are qualities to be prized in poems.

17. Cf. James W. Bright, *An Anglo-Saxon Reader* (New York 1891): "The [Maldon] poet has described this battle with the fidelity of an eye-witness. From the minuteness of details it is to be inferred that the poem was composed soon after the event" (223).

Henry Sweet's "Sketch of the History of Anglo-Saxon Poetry," prepared expressly for the fourth edition of Warton's
History, contains many of the same opinions. However, he
seems to be more appreciative of Old English poetry than
other historians. His explanation of the absence of similes is
distinctly unorthodox: "Important characteristics of Anglo-
Saxon poetry are conciseness and directness. Everything that
retards the action or obscures the main sentiment of the poem
is avoided, hence all similes are extremely rare" (Sweet 1871,
6).

A passage from Gustav Körting's *Grundriss der Geschichte
der englischen Literatur* will sufficiently illustrate his view:

> Seen absolutely, the esthetic value of the Anglo-Saxon folk
> epic is certainly not high. . . . Anglo-Saxon poetry at the time
> of its composition or reworking of the poems handed down to
> us had already ceased to live and was in the process of sinking
> to a mechanical, stereotyped level. Moreover the religious epic
> shows, in more ways than one, an insipidity, vagueness and
> mannerism, which make it appear even more distasteful to
> modern readers than the folk epic (Körting 1887, 25–26).

Stopford Brooke opens his introduction with this assessment of Old English poems: "That poetry is certainly not of a
very fine quality, but it is frequently remarkable" (Brooke
1892, v). Brooke's *History* indulges in the extremes of nineteenth-century impressionism and seeks for the "soul" of the
English race in Anglo-Saxon poems; for Brooke, this "soul" is
a cross between Wordsworth and Tennyson, and when some
quality in Old English reminds him fleetingly of these two
Romantic writers, he is pleased (vi, 214).

Courthope's *History of English Poetry* requires even less
notice than Brooke's. The poetry of Chaucer, "the fitting
starting-point of the History," has no connection with the
Anglo-Saxon (Courthope 1895, xxvii). Consequently, he has
little use for the more ancient poems. His one interesting comment remains merely provocative; he wonders why "Cynewulf
and his school [were] content to imitate the trivial subjects of
their [Latin] masters, without reflecting on the radical difference between Latin and Teutonic styles of poetry—the terseness and condensation of the hexameter, the expansion and

verbosity of alliterative verse" (104). One marvels that Old English poetry survived its discovery and revival in the hands of these earnest scholiasts.

The first half of the twentieth century produced materials on Anglo-Saxon style that were grounded squarely on the grammatical and rhetorical precepts already outlined. In remaining conservative and backward-looking the applied study of style in Old English poetry lost contact with some major theoretical innovations. For around the turn of the century, "scientific" stylistics came into the foreground, leaving the traditional categories of rhetorical analysis in a much diminished role. The impetus behind this change seems to have been, somewhat paradoxically, the emergence of an esthetic which interpreted style as an expression of an author's personality.[18] Certainly the amount of critical energy put into the definition of Cynewulf's personal style in order to establish his canon is a part of this movement. But in Anglo-Saxon studies "scientific" stylistics had a minimal effect; only in the last two decades have various contemporary derivations from the earlier theories—Formalism, New Criticism, and Structuralism—been used with any regularity in the interpretation of Old English texts.

Between the beginning of the twentieth century and the Second World War, German contributions to the study of style still overwhelm those by British and American scholars. A brief survey of Anglo-American criticism may be in order before turning to the Germans. W. P. Ker's reasonable statements remain excessively general, and they are combined with a tendency to view both Old English and Old Norse poetry as peculiarities in the greater history of medieval European literature. He writes: "The nature of the two forms of poetry is revealed in their respective manners of going wrong. The decline of the old English poetry is shown by an increase of diffuseness and insipidity" (Ker 1897, 157). Norse falls victim to

18. See Volker Kapp, "Das Stil-Konzept in den Anfängen der romanistischen Stilforschung," *In Memoriam Friedrich Diez: Akten des Kolloquiums zur Wissenschaftsgeschichte der Romanistik*, ed. Hans-Josef Niederehe and Harald Haarman, Amsterdam Studies in the Theory and History of Linguistic Science ser. 3 vol. 9 (Amsterdam 1976) 381–402.

that "familiar literary plague, the corruption of metaphor" (159).

W. W. Lawrence's warning, that it is "dangerous to depend upon subjective and *a priori* conceptions of Anglo-Saxon poetic style" (Lawrence 1906, 342), was directed mainly at the disintegrators of Müllenhoff's school. Their notions, Lawrence writes, "presuppose a high degree of smoothness and consistency and lead to elaborate and minute rearrangements of the texts" (342–43). R. W. Chambers later accuses Lawrence of a similar subjective approach to poetry (Chambers 1912, 138). But however valid such a charge may be, Lawrence at least saw that the stylistic description must be drawn from inside the poem, that poems should not be stretched on a Procrustean bed: critical standards must be appropriate to the poem (Lawrence 1906, 373).

Albert S. Cook proved himself a formidable editor and scholar; his comments on style are less impressive. He strongly resembles the appreciative and impressionistic writers of the literary histories.[19] A brief but important piece on parenthetic exclamations by G. P. Krapp deserves notice; he sees them as marks of the epic style:

> They originated in the early heroic verse, and . . . were frequently used in the later imitative verse with a sense of their epic connotation, although in general the feeling for these, as for many other, elements of the epic style became somewhat dulled and obscured in the later verse (Krapp 1905, 34).

Three British studies written by Nora Kershaw, H. C. Wyld, and E. D. Laborde in the 1920s require scrutiny more for their quirks, perhaps, than for their right-mindedness. Kershaw hits upon several salient features of Old English style, although her presuppositions are of dubious value: "It strikes us as rather strange that so abstract a type of poetry should have prevailed in an age which we are accustomed to

19. As one example, take the short quotations from *The Christ of Cynewulf* (Boston 1909): "Admirable are his graphic descriptions of arms and armor. . . . He has the poet's love for beauty" (lxxxv); "Cynewulf's sense of color is somewhat obscured . . . by his passion for light" (lxxxvii).

regard as barbarous . . . and it may be that the intellectual standard of the age was higher than is generally recognised" (Kershaw 1922, 7). She fails to see that abstraction is *per se* often a quality of "barbarous," as well as highly civilized, art. Her stylistic categories are, like many others, the result of a tendency to idealize falsely. Of *The Wife's Lament* and *The Husband's Message* she says: "the style and tone . . . are wholly different, in spite of certain similarities of diction, the one being involved, excited and desperate, while the other is simple in style and serene in tone" (41–42).

Wyld's well-known essay, "Diction and Imagery in Anglo-Saxon Poetry," harmonizes with Kershaw's account, and together they bring a new evaluation of Anglo-Saxon art and civilization:

> Not only does this ancient literature, the creation of a people formerly regarded as barbarous, exhibit arresting qualities of elevation of thought, and a sustained intensity of poetic emotion, together with great delicacy and tenderness of feeling, but the form in which it is couched is often wrought to the last pitch of elaboration, with a wealth of ornament in the shape of metaphor and pictorial phrase (Wyld 1925, 49–50).

This enthusiastic description of the Anglo-Saxon poetic vocabulary, in contrast to past condescension, explains the audience Wyld attracted. His methodology is simple and straightforward; he categorizes Old English poetic diction under three headings: "(1) distinctively poetical words and phrases. . . . (2) The figurative or metaphorical use of words, to express natural, material, objects . . . (3) What appears to be a more or less individual use of words and phrases with striking poetic effect" (53). But underneath this appearance of scheme rests a deep personalism merged with a wholly Romantic sensibility. When he says that "The old poets are fond of using the processes of nature as symbols of moods" (69), he clearly has something Wordsworthian in mind; E. G. Stanley's long essay finally divorces the study of Old English diction from such Romantic analogies (Stanley 1956, 413–66).

Without a doubt, E. D. Laborde gives us the most peculiar

stylistic analysis ever wrought upon an Old English poem. Not that *what* he writes is wrong; in fact, his technical commentary on *The Battle of Maldon* as an example of late Old English style merits a careful review. Only his conclusion need be set down here:

> To sum up, the style of Old English poetry as exemplified in *Maldon* had undergone considerable development since the early period of literature. It had outgrown the defects of irrelevance and archaism, and had almost cured itself of the obscurity due to involved parallelisms and parenthetic notes; it had lost the abruptness of immaturity only too visible in the early poems and had acquired a degree of mellowness; and it had polished up the crudities of language and syntax which abound in earlier works. . . . On the other hand, poetic style fully retained the use of variation in subject-matter, phrase, and word, and its phraseology had reached a stage of the utmost conventionality. Yet it was redeemed by its simplicity, for it used few figurative expressions, avoided the ornament of poetic allusion, contained no passages of high poetic colouring and no picturesque descriptions of nature. And in its plain, though lofty, style is perhaps seen the high-water mark of Old English narrative verse (Laborde 1924, 417).

If we were to reduce this argument to its logical extreme, we would have to conclude that *The Battle of Maldon* represents the "high-water mark" *because* it no longer contains the essential ingredients of its own style.

Anglo-American criticism is difficult to characterize because its roots go back to the belletristic tradition and the comments, as we have seen, are often personal or even whimsical. Such is certainly not the case with the German school of rhetorical and generic criticism. Though frequently mistaken, German study of Anglo-Saxon style has a rigor noticeably lacking in English and American work. Alois Brandl's long essay at the very beginning of this century in H. Paul's *Grundriss der germanischen Philologie* may stand as both model and apex of the German mode; it deserves detailed review. Brandl has not freed himself entirely from the assumptions of nineteenth-century poetics, yet the scope and clarity of his treatment command great respect. He divides all Old English poetry into six main categories—genres would be too precise a term: 1) Heathen-ritual poetry, 2) gnomic poetry, 3) commemorative verse, 4) lyric poetry, 5) epic poetry, and 6) didactic (Christian) poetry (Brandl 1901). For each type he provides a catalogue of grammatical, rhetorical, and poetic techniques. Heathen-ritual poetry comprises the charms, which use a rhetoric of direct address, inversion, and anticipation through the "preposed pronoun." He notes that the charms contain little assonance or description, and subordinate clauses and comparisons are rare. Nominal expressions replace verbs; intensifying adjectives predominate. Repetition of words and meanings within a single phrase occur frequently (quite unlike the epic style). The charms thus attain a force possible only in direct and elevated address, and not in narrative (955f.).

Gnomic poetry, on the other hand, lacks the exciting and urgent figures with which the charms are filled, as well as the variation so plentiful in epic poetry. Instead Brandl finds many series of short sentences monotonously beginning with *bið* or *sceal*. Extended descriptive passages crop up only in the gnomic poetry of *The Exeter Book*, probably under the influence of the lyric impulse. The difference between Cotton gnomes and the later *Fæder Larcwidas* (*Precepts*) is noteworthy: in the former, compounds are more vivid but less plentiful; in the latter, compounds are used mainly for more abstract, spiritual concepts. Christian education effected this change (962f.).

Commemorative verses differ significantly from the other types of Old English poems, and Brandl observes that scholars have barely begun to characterize the style of such commemorative poems as *Widsith* (965f.). (This was true in his day but much detailed work was later done by Chambers and Malone.)[20] These poems show the simplest style in the metrical line. There are no breaks in the verses, which proceed in a series of cosmological and didactic pronouncements without

20. See Chambers, and also Kemp Malone, ed., *Widsith* (London 1936).

repetition of particular phrases or rhyme, as in the charms. Lists and catalogues replace repetition. He speculates that the pragmatic nature of commemorative verse explains its close resemblance to prose, a speculation with which Malone would certainly not agree.[21]

Of the lyric poems only *Deor* exhibits a genuine strophic form; yet the original strophic underlay can be discerned in all the lyric poems (975f.). The beginning of each "strophe" is strongly marked either by placing the main concept in initial position or by a recurring word or particle. Epic avoids this trait because it interrupts the narrative flow; however, it seems suitable to the lyric, which unfolds in emotional images.

Epic poetry falls into two distinct divisions, represented by the *Finnsburg Fragment* and *Beowulf*—heroic lay and expanded epic. Dialogue in the *Fragment* tends to be short; in *Beowulf* the speeches are long. In the description of important events, the *Fragment* sketches only a few aspects; in *Beowulf* we see full descriptions of both action and setting. All this adds up to a distinction between the cryptic technique of the heroic lay versus the "broad," more expansive style of the full-blown epic. Sharp limits on variation also typify the earlier poetry, for the increase in variation seen in *Waldere* already indicates a development away from the rhapsodic lay and toward the epic. Finally, Brandl notes that the very richness of variation in certain sections of *Beowulf* illustrates that the generic evolution is complete, and not that *Beowulf* is a "composite" poem (988f.), as Müllenhoff had argued.

A narrower perspective on *Beowulf*'s rhetoric reveals the presence of all the "modest" devices of the Old Germanic epic: short comparisons, a few metaphors (sometimes elevated to puzzling kennings), elaborate compounds, ornamental adjectives usually describing a state of mind, many adverbial modifiers and oppositions within the half-line, and occasional lists (1012f.). Lyrical additions become much more prevalent, while purely descriptive techniques do not undergo further development. Christianity undoubtedly caused this intrusion of the lyrical mode in the epic, and while it led to some artistic advances, it also created an awkward mixture of styles.

21. See Malone (n. 20 above) 1–8.

The rise of Christian didactic poetry brought sweeping rhetorical changes (1025f.). New compounds were formed for abstract concepts and old compounds were suppressed to be replaced by derivative forms in *un-*, *-lic*, *-ness*, and also by descriptive genitives and adjectives. Germanic tension-creating devices (questions, exclamations, etc.) became rare; figures typical of didactic poetry (anaphora, parallel constructions) began to prevail. Extended periodic constructions and an addiction to passages of description betray the literate poet familiar with the styles of both Latin poetry and prose. Such features are clearly visible in the Cynewulfian poems, where there is an attempt to maintain the traditions of both the heroic epic and gnomic poems alongside the abstractions of Christian theology (1042f.). Cynewulf's style revels in intellectual oppositions, parallel series, and tricks of rhyme, stretching over several verses. And while every older epic begins with an emphatic sentence, *Elene* opens with a calm, periodic structure, reminiscent of Latin prose.

Christ III illustrates the final stage: epithets have nearly disappeared; the poet prefers lists and catalogues to the older variations and oppositions (1049f.). Metaphors have lost their Germanic flavor and turned into Latin imitations. Latin clerical poetry also had its effect on vernacular poetry of the later period, as seen in the emergence of end rhyme, the loss of compounds, the increase in sentence transitions, and the parallel construction of the verses (1081f.). Later critics have qualified or rejected some of Brandl's opinions, but none has surpassed his range and perspicuity in dealing with the whole diverse collection of Anglo-Saxon poems.

Walther Paetzel's study of variation, although more specialized in form, is of equal consequence (Paetzel 1913). Paetzel's treatise replaced the nineteenth-century work on this important element of Old English poetic style and remains the foundation for all modern investigations. Variation occurs when a concept, already sufficiently characterized for understanding, is brought to the attention of the listener or reader once again, often with interruption of the syntactic context. The main characteristics of variation are 1) conceptual repetition, 2) looseness of relation to the syntax of the sentence, and

3) rare occurrence in prose (3f.). Variation falls into two broad classes: 1) word variation (nouns, adjectives, and verbs) and 2) sentence variation (repetition of a thought in consecutive sentences). While Paetzel disallows two words bound by a conjunction as variation, he permits two synonymous sentences thus connected (12f.).

The repetitive quality of Old English poetry, noticed from the start of Anglo-Saxon studies, creates a number of cases where it is difficult to tell whether strict variation exists or not. Examples of such borderlines are 1) between variation and explanatory apposition (especially for proper names), 2) between variation and formulaic apposition, and 3) between variation and lists (24f.). Many of Paetzel's distinctions are intuitive and cannot be reduced to a completely rigorous system.

Relying on Heinzel's comparative methodology for stylistic analysis, Paetzel examines variation in all Germanic poetry: Old Norse has the least, Old Saxon the most, Old English occupies a middle ground (63f.). Variation has its roots in the epic style and consequently shows up most often in poems with epic content (162f.). Variations composed of more than two parts appear infrequently in Old English, and the parts which vary tend to occur in different long lines, with one or more long lines intervening. Paetzel attributes this to the growing ascendancy of *Hakenstil* ("hooked style") over *Zeilenstil* ("line style") in West Germanic (174, 177f.). Old English shows a definite preference for one-part variations, again holding a middle position between Old Norse and Old Saxon (187). The development of variation Paetzel believes moves away from the Old Norse to the Old Saxon, that is, away from variation with more than one element (for example, noun plus adjective plus genitive) toward the exclusive use of one element. Artistically speaking, this development parallels a shift from an expressive to an unexpressive use of the device (187). Paetzel finds no clear historical movement, even though the West and North Germanic styles are distinct. Nor can the age or author of a text be determined from the use of variation (214f.).

Later work has modified Paetzel's initial survey of this stylistic phenomenon. Arthur G. Brodeur, for example, maintains that variations need not be parallel in structure as well as in meaning: "Identity of sense is more essential to variation than identity of structure" (Brodeur 1960, 41). Brodeur insists that the important point is to distinguish between variation, enumeration and progression. In strict variation, which he defines as "a double or multiple statement of the same concept or idea in different words, with a more or less perceptible shift in stress" (40), each member of the sequence must have the identical referent (41). Fred C. Robinson returns to Paetzel's tenet that identity of structure is a basic requirement for variation, and his new terminology has helped to clarify some of the discriminations blurred in Paetzel's account. For Robinson, *variation* refers to the total construction; *components* stand for the various members of that construction, with *variatum* applying to the first component and *varians* to the second and all subsequent components (Robinson 1961).

The connection Paetzel makes between the development of variation and the rise of *Hakenstil* leads logically to a discussion of "enjambment" in Old English poetry. One poem—*Be Domes Dæge* or *Judgment Day II*—did much to confuse early scholars on this question. A very close translation of a Latin model, *Be Domes Dæge* was known to be of late vintage. Since it imitates the Latin source precisely, all the ends of sentences occur at ends of full verse lines. Deutschbein completely misinterpreted this fact and believed that *Hakenstil* was the original form of Germanic verse, and that *Zeilenstil* gained more and more ground as time went on (Deutschbein 1902, 25–27). He sees this "change" accurately enough as due to a greater dependence on Latin models, but goes astray when he calls it a decay in the art of Old English poetry (25). His conclusions are taken over by Schwarz, who employs them for his own purposes in analyzing Cynewulf's authorship of *Christ* (Schwarz 1905, 85f.). Although Schwarz uses faulty premises, he reaches what is now the accepted position—*Christ II* is by Cynewulf, *Christ I* and *III* are not (103).

At the time that Deutschbein and Schwarz were writing, a different opinion came from A. Heusler who regarded *Zeilenstil* as definitely the more archaic and the less artistic (Heusler

1902, 235f.). Heusler later expanded his brief notice into a full study of the two styles (Heusler 1920, 1–48). He finds that the earlier West Germanic epic, represented by the *Finnsburg Fragment*, had moved from strophic form to the use of *Zeilenstil*. But end-stopped lines had already been abandoned by the oldest of the religious epics (*Genesis A*) in favor of *Hakenstil*. This style with its deliberate tension between metrical and syntactical borders gives the feeling of greater motion, for when the sentence ends, the line is often only half-completed and vice versa (9f.). However, the style did not gain ground steadily in Old English epics; *Daniel* returns to *Zeilenstil* and represents an intermediate step between *Finnsburg* and *Waldere* or *Beowulf*, all of which depend less on *Hakenstil* than *Genesis*. Cynewulf is very inconsistent: *Juliana* has proportions similar to *Beowulf*; *Elene* is very close to the verse style of the *Heliand* (10). With this discontinuous development, no responsible critic can use the ratio of *Zeilenstil* to *Hakenstil* as a test of age; the older traditions held their own, while the religious poets sometimes explored new stylistic possibilities (11). Two side-effects accompany the emergence of *Hakenstil*—an increase in variation and a turn to hypotaxis. Both of these follow from the looser patterns created by enjambment (16f.).

The clearest brief in the debate over end-stopped and run-on lines in relation to the chronology of Old English poems comes from Kemp Malone. His analysis deserves full illustration:

> In general, a plurilinear unit of classical OE poetry was held together, not by uniformities of rhythmical or alliterative pattern, nor yet by uniformities of grouping (i.e. strophic structure), but by the use of run-on lines. . . . We further distinguish three stages in the development of the run-on style in OE poetry. The early stage is exemplified in the amnemonic parts of *Widsith* (the mnemonic parts exemplify the end-stopped style . . .). Here the plurilinear units vary in number of lines, but this variation is held within comparatively narrow limits: no unit longer than nine lines occurs. All the natural divisions of the poem end with a line; not one ends with an onverse (i.e. in the middle of a line). Single lines and couplets

make a respectable proportion of the whole. Most of the run-on lines are of the second kind mentioned above; that is, they end with a syntactical pause, though not with a full stop. *Beowulf* may serve to illustrate the middle stage of the run-on style. Here some of the plurilinear units are of great length; their length may be so great, indeed, that they no longer can be felt as units and include diverse matters. Single lines and couplets are infrequent. . . . *Judith* exemplifies the late stage of the run-on style. Here one can hardly speak of plurilinear units at all, or indeed of clear-cut units of any kind, apart from the fits (Malone 1943, 202–03).

To this date no critic has improved on Malone's dictum.

These works on variation are restricted in their range. Shortly after Paetzel's copious study of this figure, Ludwig Wolff chose to make an unrestricted survey of Old English stylistic devices. As the title of his article, "Über den Stil der altgermanischen Poesie," suggests, Wolff's essay is both an update and a correction of Heinzel (Wolff 1923, 214). Relying heavily on Heusler and Paetzel, Wolff attempts to divorce the peculiarities of Germanic style from an Indo-European base and to find an organic relationship among all the different stylistic qualities of Germanic poetry, as well as to isolate the local and particular developments which took place in each of the tribes. Alliteration is not for Wolff just a mechanical trick, as rhyme and stanza form sometimes are in decadent periods of literature (215). The alliteration and the poetic effect work together in perfect symbiosis. Wolff devotes most of his piece to a discussion of variation and the proportions of *Zeilenstil* and *Hakenstil* in the various Germanic literatures. Again his approach is to find the organic connection between stylistic traits. Appositions and synonyms naturally lead to *heiti*, kennings and formal variation (215f.), the predominance of kennings or variation produces either the strophic form with *Zeilenstil* (Old Norse) or the loose verse paragraph with *Hakenstil* (West Germanic) (217f.).

Wolff complains, with justification, that the term *kenning* had not been defined precisely. Bode's early work on the subject was mainly a catalogue. Wolff insists on two important points about kennings: 1) they must have two parts, and 2) they share the character of the paraphrase. A kenning should be perceived as a substitute for a simple term, and such a paraphrase only occurs when the simple and unpoetic term must be avoided for the sake of variation. Thus Wolff draws a distinction between the kenning and variation: the kenning has universal significance and typifies, while variation presents individual characteristics that "vivify" the context. The kenning is self-sufficient and would be weakened if it were included in a variation, which, in fact, rarely happens (217).

More elaborate studies of the kenning appeared in 1929 and 1938. Van der Merwe Scholtz agrees with many of his forerunners that the influence of Christianity accounts for the relative absence of kennings and metaphors in Old English poetry. The Christian outlook supposedly changed the natural Germanic bent from figurative vitality to somber reflection, a "subjective" attitude, and moral seriousness (van der Merwe Scholtz 1929, 26f.). Formally speaking, van der Merwe Scholtz finds no difference between the kenning and the *heiti* (38). He writes: "it would . . . be more correct to regard kenningar as words and phrases used in a figurative *or* a specialized, as opposed to the literal *or* general sense of such words and phrases" (47). He, too, sees the origin of the kenning "in its earlier use as variation, when it could accompany, but not supplant, the name of the person or object to which it refers" (108). In addition, kennings developed from "free copulations or occasional kenningar," and those constructed by derivation (139).

Van der Merwe Scholtz's work on kennings is neither as systematic nor as penetrating as Hertha Marquardt's monograph which appeared nine years later. Marquardt criticizes earlier studies of the kenning for being little more than lists, without analysis or interpretations (Marquardt 1938, 104–07). She divides her own study into two sections, a theoretical portion, and a taxonomic description of kennings according to the paraphrased concept. First Marquardt reviews the complex attempts that had been made to define the kenning. She herself does not try to arrive at a new overall definition, but assimilates the acceptable portions of those previous critics had offered, while insisting that a full treatment must include both poem and context. Her conclusions are multifarious: the base word may or may not be close in meaning to the entire concept expressed by the kenning (120). When it is close, the other member of the two-part phrase must further particularize in order for that sequence to qualify as a kenning. Usually the base word is not the main concept, but a partial image from which the whole is constructed. Marquardt claims that the base word usually presents only one essential side of the paraphrased concept. In Old English the meaning of the paraphrase often depends on the context. As for the modifying word, the less colorful or more abstract the base word, the more meaning the modifier gains, so that certain types of paraphrases are mainly characterized only by the modifying word. A tension, more or less perceptible, always exists between the base word and the modifier.

Kennings can be both expanded and abbreviated; Old English has the potential to form three-part kennings, though these are exceptional. The shortened kenning lacks the modifying word, but it is obvious from the context what that modifier would be (154–56). Kennings are independent of the sentence context and can be inserted at any convenient place; sentences themselves may serve as an explanation of a kenning (gnomic verse). Within the sentence, a kenning may replace any part normally occupied by a noun, or it may stand in apposition to a noun.

In the second section, Marquardt lists the main categories of kennings by content: nature, the world of man, peoples, Christian concepts. Examination of content is particularly important for the Old English kenning, as this often provides the only way to determine whether an expression is a kenning or not (160). Marquardt does not agree with Wolff on the relation between variation and the kenning. She believes variation is the main stylistic trait of Old English poetry; the kenning can be included in variation, but it need not be bound to the variation—nor is variation dependent on the kenning (308).

Two possibilities exist for the relation between the meaning of the kenning and the meaning of the sentence; they may agree with one another, or stand in contrast. In the first instance, she chooses the term "appropriate," *treffende* (308f.); most Old English kennings fit this description. A completely unambiguous opposition between kenning and context occurs very rarely (309). Still one cannot assume that all kennings were *treffende*. Many were used as formulae with little or no attention paid to the literal meaning, although this tends to happen only when overuse has drained the kenning of its literal signification (311).

Through its literal and figurative meanings, the kenning functions as a poetic elevation, an intensifier of the simple concept. The poet places one essential aspect of this idea in the foreground and makes it into a self-contained image. Kennings are used only for significant notions since they comprise the high point of the sentence; kennings also play a valuable role in variation. Both stylistic features work in the same direction of intensifying expression (311f.).

Marquardt observes that purely descriptive portions of poems do not contain kennings. Since kennings stress the essence rather than the external form of an object, they are unsuitable for this purpose. Likewise kennings serve no useful purpose in objective narrative, since they belong to an "elevated" level of poetic diction and mirror the poet's subjective attitude (313).

German criticism of the first third of the twentieth century dealt primarily with isolated figures, tropes, but not schemes. In *The Larger Rhetorical Patterns in Anglo-Saxon Poetry*, Adeline Courtney Bartlett succeeds in removing these restrictive parameters and in mapping new directions for the study of style. Acknowledging her debt to Hoffman (1883), she remarks at the conclusion of her study:

> The attempt in the foregoing chapters has been to follow Hoffmann's theory a part of the way, at least, and to insist upon this rhetorically developed style which, in its most finished form, was the peculiar property of the Anglo-Saxon poetry. The task, in particular, has been to show the rhetorical building up of long poetic passages, and the fixing of specific long rhetorical patterns (Bartlett 1935, 113).

Bartlett treats several rhetorical features, but her most influential chapter deals with the "Envelope pattern," which consists of "any logically unified group of verses bound together by the repetition at the end of (1) words or (2) ideas or (3) words and ideas which are employed at the beginning" (9). The "whole passage is a decorative inset, description apparently for its own sake imposed upon the narrative" (16). She insists that the "content of an Envelope group is always a logical unit . . . a conscious unit, consciously designed" (18), one which bears out her premise that in Old English verse paragraphs the rhetorical unit dominates the metrical unit (6). Envelope patterns develop "out of a chiastic arrangement" (19), perhaps related to what Heinzel described as ABA order or to ten Brink's "intersecting moments" (20 and 108). Such a compositional mode implies two things: the repetition so frequently censured by earlier critics now constitutes a viable pattern—interlace has become respectable; similarly, the static quality of the Old English poem ceases to be a defect, for the "cumulative effect of all these [rhetorical] patterns and devices is to emphasize the non-narrative feeling of Anglo-Saxon 'epic'" (108). Bartlett is certainly not the first to propose that the formal laws of Old English poetry may have their own intrinsic validity, but her work delineated some of those rules with such effectiveness that contemporary stylistic criticism still relies, implicitly or explicitly, on her fundamental principles.

Gavin Bone's essay on Old English, written at the beginning of the 1940s, defies classification. Highly eccentric, abounding in *sensibilité*, the preface to his own translations stands by itself in the long history of stylistic criticism. While he shares with countless others an aversion to the saints' lives and other didactic pieces (Bone 1943, 25), his comments on the Anglo-Saxon language and its relation to poetic imagery have value despite their curious preciosity:

> The first unusual fact which imposes itself on the student of Anglo-Saxon poetry is the portmanteau descriptive phrase: an attempt to include in the name of the thing as much as possible of the thing itself. . . . This method of the gripped epithet (the noun holding another noun or adjective in a vice, so that it can't get away but shares its life with the noun and forms a compound name) is carried farther in Anglo-Saxon poetry than in any other poetry we are likely to know (11–12).

The scops "have not got musical thought" (14). Yet he finds that "Anglo-Saxon is a nice strong vigorous language for writing poetry. The words are stony and have character, and there is the great advantage in Anglo-Saxon verse that it is impossible to be neat. . . . The Anglo-Saxon poets are well free of the tyranny of the epigram, the insolence of the paradox" (24). Here is a modern poet's intensely personal response to Old English verse; it is unfortunate that Bone did not live to write more on the subject.

Nearly all the scholarly work done in the 1940s concentrated on syntax, starting with S. O. Andrew's controversial book on *Syntax and Style.* Andrew's main premise may be simply put: "the supposed 'paratactic' structure of Old English, whether in prose or verse, is an illusion" (Andrew 1940, n.p.). What others have labelled parataxis, Andrew claims, is actually asyndetic coordination (72). Assuming that parataxis is the main syntactical feature of Old English, critics have believed that the epic style, especially in *Beowulf,* is "archaic or primitive"; Andrew argues that "there could be no greater delusion" (94). Most of his book is taken up with specific analyses, after which he concludes: "Nothing in fact is left of the supposed paratactic style; except for the occasional use of idiomatic parataxis, itself as we have seen . . . a subordinating device, the prevailing sentence-structure is not paratactic at all but periodic" (108). The academic establishment did not welcome Andrew's declarations, and has nearly rejected his more extreme views put forth in a later book on *Beowulf* (Andrew 1948).

Claes Schaar makes the distinction between parataxis and hypotaxis his touchstone in fixing the canon of Cynewulf's poems (Schaar 1949, 153–72). Schaar represents the culmination of the long and productive Germanic tradition; he searches for those differences in style among the poems which demonstrate conclusively the psychological traits identifying a particular author (9). He clings to the notion that Old English poetic style consists of "repetitions, digressions, vagueness and frequent inconsistencies," but he refuses to accept "the application of cut and dried logical standards" (47). Schaar turns to the vast literature on the Cynewulf canon and finds it wanting because it has depended almost exclusively on descriptive catalogues with "no systematic comparison and no real analysis" (97). The following passage contains his impressions of past studies and the aims of his own:

> What is striking in most of the works surveyed . . . is the almost impressive optimism on the part of the scholars as to the possibility of solving a problem of attribution by drawing extensive conclusions from a few isolated details chosen at random and without regard to critical principles. Few of the scholars have asked themselves the necessary question: What features of an author's style and manner are so personal to him that similar features in a certain text indicate it as being his work, or that the absence of these features in another text prevents it from being attributed to him? . . . The objective of our stylistic study . . . is to find and analyse 1) features of the style . . . which we may suppose to be stamped by the poets' individualities to a greater extent than other features; 2) features which we may suppose to be due to traditional influence. . . . When dealing with the features belonging to the first group, we shall first concentrate on those elements in a poet's style that are indicative of his capacity for distinguishing between vital and subordinate epic matter. . . . We can decide to what extent such distinctions are made when we analyse the use of . . . compound and complex clause-series. On a minor scale the ability to distinguish between essential and subordinate matter is apparent from an author's way of expressing causal relations: he may subordinate cause to effect or he may put both on the same level. The capacity referred to may also be judged from the extent to which an author expresses incidents vital to the plot in subordinate clauses. These two points will be treated in the chapter on causal parataxis and essential hypotaxis. . . . We also see a more or less highly developed discriminative talent in the extent to which an author stresses unimportant elements of a sentence by means of variation (113–15).

Schaar's analyses are meticulous and exhaustive although some of his categories maintain certain preconceptions not entirely sympathetic to the nature of Anglo-Saxon style. Nonetheless, limiting the Cynewulf canon to the "signed" poems has been an unchallenged practice ever since his study.

A rebuttal to some of Schaar's methods was not long in forthcoming. Alarik Rynell attacks the syntactical portions of Schaar's book with special force. In this attack he challenges the whole premise that syntax evolves from a primitive parataxis to a sophisticated hypotaxis. He points out "how hard it is to draw a sharp line of demarcation between parataxis and hypotaxis," and reminds us that "most scholars seem to agree that some kind of hypotaxis occurred even in Indo-European" (Rynell 1952, 4, 24).

Rynell also warns against making value judgments based on a simplistic distinction between these two syntactic categories:

> If modern prose-writers can be praised for using parataxis, how could we blame ancient poets for using this type of sentence structure, which is, on the whole, more natural to poetry, and which was particularly so at a time when poetry was largely founded on oral tradition and intended for oral delivery, when hypotaxis in its most obvious form, characterized by the use of introductory or connective words of subordination, was not very highly developed, partly because language was less exposed to foreign (Latin) influence than it was later to be, when, finally, what we now take to be parataxis was often rather an early form of hypotaxis (47)?

Schaar's conclusions remain intact, despite Rynell's serious questioning of his methods.

Rynell's allusion to oral tradition introduces the major stylistic concern of the 1950s: literary historians had long known that formulaic repetitions occur in Old English poetry, but it was not until Magoun's dogmatic pronouncements that the formula was elevated to a position as base unit of all poetic composition (Magoun 1953, 446–63).[22] Following the investigations of Milman Parry and Albert Lord into Homeric and contemporary Yugoslavian oral traditions (Lord 1969), Magoun asserts: "Oral poetry . . . is composed entirely of formulas,

---

22. One should note, however, that Albert B. Lord in *The Singer of Tales* (Cambridge Mass. 1969) takes pains to point out that he, in his 1948 Harvard dissertation, was the first scholar to aply the Parry-Lord hypothesis to Old English poetry (198).

large and small, while lettered poetry is never formulaic, though lettered poets occasionally consciously repeat themselves or quote verbatim from other poets in order to produce a specific rhetorical or literary effect" (Magoun 1953, 447).

The extensions of this idea have serious ramifications: if one assumes that all Old English poetry is formulaic, then, in Magoun's terms, it must also be the product of an oral tradition. Oral poetry has no fixed text until transcribed; an oral poem is an abstraction assumed to exist as a base structure for all the performances of that poem through an unknown number of years, generations, or even centuries. Conventional literary criticism buckles before such a concept of poetic composition, and Magoun argues that for this reason one cannot describe the "style" of an Old English poem (461). Robert P. Creed amplifies Magoun's negative position. He suggests that an entirely new kind of criticism must be developed to handle Old English poetry, one that will take the formulae and analyze them not only in their immediate contexts, but also in the context of the history of that formula both within the poem and with an eye to the tradition *in toto* (Creed 1961).

Magoun's opinions have spawned a vast literature. Questions concerning dictation, literate poets, transitional texts, themes, type-scenes, and ring composition have great import for the criticism of Old English poetry. But Magoun's original dogmatism has defined the responses of his critics, so that the discussion continues mainly on the theoretical level, with constant attempts to define and redefine the terms.[23] Consequently, the actual stylistic criticism that the oral-formulaicists have produced tends to be statistical and self-serving. One does not have to agree with Haarder's dictum that oral-formulaic criticism is boring and finally unrevealing (Haarder 1975, 199) to see that this significant discovery, with its over-positive assumptions has, in fact, inhibited literary analysis.

The most successful use of the oral-formulaic theory for stylistic studies has come from those scholars who do not have a personal investment in maintaining or refining Magoun's

23. An excellent summary of the controversy may be found in Andreas Haarder, *Beowulf: The Appeal of a Poem* (Aarhus 1975) 178–204.

hypotheses. An especially discriminating critique is Stanley B. Greenfield's. He asks:

> If, then, individual words and even conventional epithets could be used with precision, metaphoric aptness and aesthetic effectiveness in Old English poetry, is it possible that under certain circumstances formulas in larger formal patterns or associations could exhibit nuances or extensions of meaning such as we have come to expect in the patterns of modern poetry? (Greenfield 1972, 52)

Greenfield's detailed and subtle analyses answer his own rhetorical question in the affirmative; the existence of oral formulas in Old English poetry does not invalidate or prevent literary effect. As Greenfield says, formulaic echoes "make their own stylistic contributions" to these poems (58). The debate set in motion by Magoun has hardly begun to subside; what seems most desirable would be a greater assimilation of the acceptable parts of the theory into a practical criticism, something which Greenfield has already begun.[24]

Apart from oral-formulaic theory, several valuable contributions to stylistic studies have appeared in the last twenty years. Some pursue issues raised by the Germanic school; others derive from the new schools of criticism and linguistics. E. G. Stanley's essay on poetic diction reverses many of the neo-Romantic assumptions about Old English poetry that Wyld had expressed most forcefully. Beginning with the premise that for "some OE. figurative diction . . . it is not possible to be sure if the figure was not as real to the Anglo-Saxons as the reality that gave rise to the figure" (Stanley 1956, 414), Stanley confronts the question of realism in Old English metaphors directly, and determines that "much of what appears factual in Old English verse is not truly factual" (432). He postulates a reversal of the "Wordsworthian" model that had dominated older criticism:

> Few will deny that with the old poets the processes of nature may be symbols of their moods: but it is not the flower that

24. See also Patrick W. Conner, "Schematization of Oral-Formulaic Processes in Old English Poetry," *Language and Style* 5 (1972) 204–20.

gives the thought; with the OE poets it is the thought that gives the flower. And the flower that is born of the mood may take on sufficient concreteness to appear capable of existence without and outside the mood (427).

Stanley's formulation is significant not only for the understanding of the stylistic unit *per se*; it also sharply limits a literalistic criticism by demonstrating that the diction exists independent of any specific "real" situation or emotion.

Arthur G. Brodeur's analysis of the diction of *Beowulf* proceeds on a different set of assumptions and with different goals: Brodeur wishes to overturn Magoun's assertion that the oral-formulaic quality of the poetry prohibits conventional literary discussion. His extensive treatment of compounds in *Beowulf* points toward poetic individuality rather than conformity:

> It is surprising how many compounds appear with marked infrequency. Of the various compounds found on a single base-word, a very great many are restricted to a single poem each, or at most are shared by two poems. This raises the question whether the majority of poets may not have permitted themselves a good deal of originality in the formation of compounds, and whether tradition may not have supplied merely the basic patterns on which compounds could be acceptably formed (Brodeur 1960, 34).

Magoun counters that Brodeur's data are open to a quite different interpretation (Magoun 1961, 282); but in a later article, Brodeur presses the topic of stylistic individuality even farther. In some ways Brodeur has roots in very old traditions; he sees a similarity between the description of winter in *Andreas* and the poetry of Keats; and despite Stanley's argument, he still talks about realism in descriptive passages (Brodeur 1968, 103). Brodeur raises more interesting questions than he answers. His intuitions are keen, while his methodology is weak. Thus as recently as 1968 the debate over originality of style and diction within the framework of a conventional and formulaic poetic system remained unresolved. Brodeur may be correct; yet surely one of the tasks that the stylistic analysis of Old English poetry must undertake is to find more precise means of identifying and describing what constitutes such originality.

Two related articles by Jackson J. Campbell also cast doubt on Magoun's absolutism by demonstrating that

> The Latin Christian tradition offered not only theological and philosophical doctrine, pious story material and a new purpose for poetry, but also a poetic, complete with advice on stylistic features. Factors of style the Old English poet could adopt and assimilate to his traditional Germanic verse form fully as easily as he had assimilated Christian stories to the native societal patterns (J. Campbell 1967, 2).

The "age-old formulas could easily find themselves imbedded in sophisticated poetic structures learned from Latin poets and rhetoricians" (J. Campbell 1966, 192). Campbell illustrates persuasively that devices from the Latin rhetorical tradition became an integral part of Old English style. His prescription for future studies parallels Brodeur's in several respects: "Criticism of all Old English poetry should therefore be wary, for in many formulaic poems a conscious rhetorical artificer is at work" (201). Much more work remains to be done in following the directions pointed by Brodeur and Campbell.

New perspectives on old material thoroughly worked over by German scholars appear in A. Campbell's search for an answer to the question of "why the short lay was replaced by the full-style epic" (A. Campbell 1962, 13). Campbell distinguishes between lay and epic style using the criterion of "amplitude." He doubts that research into Indo-European origins will bear fruit. Campbell thinks "independent native development with hints from classical sources" (23) can explain Old English epic style. He writes:

> That the epic style matched its fuller deployment of material with more ample paragraphs than the lay had ever known is practically certain, though adequate material for comparison is lacking. It is impossible to conceive of a style suited to the brief narrative of the lays carrying long paragraphs, carefully built with a variety of sub-clauses, such as are easily found in the Old English epics (19–20).

Campbell finds "the elaborate development of the art of parallelism" is the crucial test for distinguishing the new epic style from the old style of the lays (20); he holds that scale of treatment, not relative length, is the criterion on which such distinction rests (24).

We recall that many nineteenth-century German or German-trained critics characterized Old English style as "subjective," as opposed to the "objective" style of Old Norse. Approximately a century later G. Storms examines the "subjective emotional coloring" of compounds in *Beowulf*, namely, "those senses that are not permanent or inherent in the word but that are added by the contextual situation or produced by an emotional tone (G. Storms, 1963, 174). Storms's semantic study offers another sophisticated rebuttal to the oral-formulaicists; with Brodeur, he insists that "the poet of *Beowulf* selected his words carefully and purposively and that the exigencies of alliteration did not hamper his creative artistry" (183). The "associative richness" of the language in *Beowulf* deserves a complete examination (186). Storms also directs some of his criticism against the pat conclusions of German scholars:

> Klaeber's observations on the style of *Beowulf* are a curious mixture of sensitive appreciation and lack of full understanding (p. lxiii). His remarks on the emotional character of the style are perfectly true, but when he says that characterizing adjectives are less prominent . . . we must disagree: the . . . adjectives appeal as much to the imagination as to sentiment and moral sense (183).

Storms's objection to the explanation of stylistic effects solely on the basis of alliteration and meter is shared by A. L. Binns; but Binns's comments on passages in *Beowulf* offer new modes of perceiving Old English style based on contemporary linguistic theory (Binns 1966). He paraphrases *Beowulf*, lines 333–35 and then asks: "What is the difference between saying 'Whence do you bring your plated shields, grey mail-shirts, masked helmets, group of war spears?' and 'Whence did you come . . . with your plated shields etc. etc. etc.?'" (126). Since he insists that all differences in syntax imply a different "analysis of experience," he answers his question as follows:

> The second version starts with the subject-verb nexus and adds on the modifiers outside this. The first builds them into the nexus itself and not by any technique of subordinating adverbial or adjectival clauses.
>
> This has one rather odd consequence. A sort of 'free space' is created, a position in the sentence in which word substitution over a fairly wide range can take place without alteration in what one might call the prose meaning of the sentence. . . . This absence of techniques of grammatical subordination . . . is of course connected with the question of parataxis in Old English (127).

His main position is that Old English syntax (and the "free space" it permits) demarcates the true characteristics of the poetic style, which "keeps everything on the same line and resolutely refuses to analyse [any] phenomenon into kernel and adjectival trimmings" (128–29).

Randolph Quirk's article, "Poetic Language and Old English Metre" (1963), based on the theories of J. R. Firth, presents another linguistic approach to style (Quirk 1968). Quirk emphasizes the importance of lexical collocation within the context of the alliterative style. While he cautions that

> formulaic utterances and habitual collocations are the necessary starting point in the study of the early alliterative poetry, they are *only* the starting point. The very fact that he could depend on his audience having a firm expectation of certain dependences and determined sequences involving metre, vocabulary, and grammar gave the poet his opportunity to stretch linguistic expression beyond the ordinary potentialities of prose, and to achieve a disturbing and richly suggestive poetry (19).

All the elements of the style work together to reproduce such "stretching": variation plays a particularly important role, since "variation encourages extended collocation and at the same time allows the collocation to proceed beyond the two alliteratively bound units (3). The recurrent collocations permit the words in Old English poetry to "interanimate" each other (5) and to effect an ironic stance through "the poet's elaborately equivocal use of familiar formulas" (17). Quirk's topological approach leads to a critical explanation of the pervasive irony inherent in the style itself.

Eugene Kintgen attacks a related problem—not formulae which naturally call up others, but "echoic repetition" of the formulae themselves. Kintgen may not hit the mark when he asserts that few have seen this device as "a basic characteristic of the Old English poetic style" (Kintgen 1974, 204). John O. Beaty touches upon the phenomenon (Beaty 1934); and James L. Rosier renames it "generative composition" (Rosier 1964, 366). And, of course, repetition has always been one of the most noticed (if also most depreciated) stylistic qualities in Old English poetry; but Kintgen sees repetition as an intrinsic aspect of the Anglo-Saxon poetic system. He finds four classes of verbal echo: 1) simple repetition; 2) echoes in "which one or both of the echoing elements is part of a compound"; 3) echoes "between two etymologically related and phonetically similar elements"; 4) echoes "composed of those which combine the characteristics of the compound and the etymological echoes" (Kintgen 1974, 205-07). Syntactic and narrative repetitions form equally significant components of the system. Kintgen's study is a prolegomenon to a further investigation; he does not go much beyond this classification and the notation that "more echoes produce a denser texture" (209).[25] Still his outline provides a preliminary rationale which helps to redeem repetition in Anglo-Saxon verse.

A final linguistic item: Lydia Fakundiny, using Kuhn's law of the relative importance of sentence-particles, shows that the Old English poets achieved a large degree of fluidity by emphasizing particles not normally expected to receive stress. Rather than being trapped by "set verbal patterns and a rigid metrical hierarchy" (Fakundiny 1970, 266), the scops had considerable freedom. Fakundiny decides that "the artistry of OE. alliterative poetry relies . . . on flexibility of word order and metrical value perceived in relation to underlying norms of syntax and stress" (266).

In very recent years scholars have enlarged the boundaries

25. On texture as a stylistic feature of Old English poetry, see also Pamela Gradon, *Form and Style in Early English Literature* (London 1971) 19f.

NB

for stylistic analysis of Old English poetry. Fred C. Robinson proves how narrowly Old English lexicographers defined the semantic and metaphoric capability of the language. He observes that, judging from dictionary entries, lexicographers assume "synaesthetic metaphor to be uncharacteristic of OE poetic style. But," he adds, "the judgement seems hasty. . . . Actually, the Anglo-Saxon poets appear to have been unusually bold in their use of synaesthetic imagery" (Robinson 1970, 106). Or to take another instance, previous critics have denied that paronomasia occurs in Old English verse. Robinson comments: "The basis for this assumption is hard to determine, for paronomasia was a favorite device among the writers most familiar to the Anglo-Saxons, and the OE writers themselves discussed and used puns both in their vernacular and in their Latin writings" (107). His own researches into onomastics (Robinson 1968 [2]) and the investigations of Roberta Frank dispel this prejudice. Frank even declares that much of Old English style was "etymological," full of wordplay, though "such wordplay seems to represent the innovative, untypical aspects of a poetic tradition more often cited and revered for its conventional nature (Frank 1972, 222, 226).

The relation of style to meaning receives an especially subtle analysis in Peter Clemoes's lecture, *Rhythm and Cosmic Order in Old English Christian Literature*. Clemoes's perceptions do not reduce to a simple scheme. He views Old English "terms of expression" as "nuclei of meaning, symbols of integrated experience, aggregates of traditional associations rather than words delimited intellectually, as is most of our present-day vocabulary" (Clemoes 1970, 6). And he probes the manner in which the traditional alliterative meter corresponds to "both the narrative surface and its deep undercurrents of meaning" (8). In *The Dream of the Rood* the poet employs his half-lines antithetically to reveal the central paradox of the poem—the divinity and the humanity of Christ united in "the stylistic form of the *communicatio idiomatum*. . . . Rhythm shores up the allegorical depths of the language" (8, 11).[26] Clemoes then turns to *Christ II* and discusses Cynewulf's creation of outward

26. As Clemoes notes, the term *Communicatio idiomatum* was first

pattern through manipulation of traditional rhythm (11). However, Clemoes's concept of rhythm is not restricted to technical details; the significance of his study goes well beyond scansion to the perception that "Rhythm made language part of the ordered allegory of life. Through rhythm, first in poetry and then in prose, the English language was attuned to the medieval conception of congruity" (24). Clemoes here moves the study of style up from the surface data to the embodiment of a world view.

A major departure from conventional categories of stylistic description occurs in the work of those critics who seek analogies between Old English poetry and other arts. John Leyerle connects the complex interlace design found in Anglo-Saxon art of the seventh and eighth centuries with both the style and the structure of Anglo-Latin and Old English poems (Leyerle 1967). Peter Schroeder extends Leyerle's original idea and examines the philosophical ramifications of this stylistic comparison. He equates the use of space in Anglo-Saxon art to the use of time in Old English narrative: "Both art and poetry seem to embody the same kind of aesthetic impulse—an impulse toward abstraction rather than naturalism, an obsession with intricate design at the expense of realistic representation" (Schroeder 1974, 197). In several articles Alain Renoir has probed the relation between Anglo-Saxon poetry and cinematographic techniques. About *Judith* he writes: "the method whereby the poet moves through space and time, and shifts the point of view of his narrative, is one that can be best understood through the analogy of the cinematograph. . . . [In *Judith*], as with the cinematograph, the important thing is the visual element" (Renoir 1962, 150). And Robert Burlin finds an analogy between the Old English *Advent* and music; he claims that this poem "is a large scale composition, built up of smaller quasi-independent units and organized upon 'musical principles'" (Burlin 1968, 48f.). These analogical approaches to style are new and, perhaps, more suggestive than critical in

---

applied to *The Dream of the Rood* by Rosemary Woolf, "Doctrinal Influences on *The Dream of the Rood*," *Medium Aevum* 27 (1958) 137–53.

any stringent sense. Nonetheless such speculative ventures have supplied necessary antidotes to some of the more statistical trends in the scholarship, particularly those that have flowed from the pens of the oral-formulaicists.

An inquiring and open-ended methodology for Old English stylistics begins to emerge. The great descriptive and taxonomic endeavors of the late nineteenth and early twentieth centuries, which more or less supplanted the curious antipathies of the very first critics, are now themselves giving way to new models. R. F. Leslie's short article on the "Analysis of Stylistic Devices and Effects in Anglo-Saxon Literature" proves "that the stylistic features of Old English poetry are not merely decorative, but have an important functional part in the total structure"; and, he argues, "the syntactical constructions in their turn are diversified to suit the requirements of the style" (Leslie 1959, 135–36).

The most inclusive survey of Old English style has come from Stanley B. Greenfield, whose topics are too varied to fit neatly into this brief introduction. Greenfield relies heavily on the positive contributions of the New Criticism, combined with a thorough grounding in Germanic scholarship. He attacks the reductiveness of all critical schools that inevitably hamper a fully developed esthetic awareness. Unlike so many documents in the history of stylistic criticism, Greenfield's book invites us to see Anglo-Saxon poetry as literature, valuable in itself and with its own artful codes. Since his treatment of the poetry is specific, pragmatic, and often argumentative, I can only suggest the book's scope by referring to its topics—diction, formula, variation, sound and sense, verse form, syntax and meaning, genre. Explicit in his program is a wish to deliver stylistic criticism from much of its history:

> The interpretation of Old English *poems*—not *poetry*. One of my basic tenets is that some of the main streams of modern Old English criticism tend to detract from the special nature, the unique identity, of particular poems. This is not to deny a poem's participation in the community and commonality of its Anglo-Saxon poetical and cultural heritage, but rather . . . to make that text speak to us across the years with the dignity and self-assurance of its individuality (Greenfield 1972, ix).

The problem with which we started is not the problem with which we end: nearly three hundred years have passed between Hickes and Greenfield. But the puzzle is not yet solved; we require a broader knowledge of all the stylistic conventions before each Old English poem becomes indeed unique.

The essays collected here come out of this long, often unfocussed, and sometimes confused tradition. We do not possess a well-defined poetic which would tell us all we need to know about style in Old English poetry; there are not even any boundaries set to the investigation. So we return to Ohmann's words: "Style is a *way* of doing *it*." Each of the following contributions explores one aspect of Anglo-Saxon style; none attempts to treat the field as a whole. In their explorations, each uses a different technique for discovery, and reaches a different conclusion about the possibility of defining that style. The value of the collection lies in the interaction of these various techniques and diverse perspectives of their authors on a single subject. E. G. Stanley's essay employs the methods of historical philology to open up questions of interpretation. His emphasis is primarily on language and semantics, but his search for the verifiable meanings of Old English phrases leads him to important analyses of figurative language, metaphor, and irony in Anglo-Saxon poetry, topics which have always been at the center of stylistic study. Although Stanley doubts we will ever know enough to recapture the precise signification of Old English terms, the proof of his negative case establishes a way of obtaining positive results when the linguistic and cultural data are sufficient. Stanley B. Greenfield offers a full examination of many techniques of style through his translations. He begins his work by taking some of the qualities of Old English poetic style as given, and then incorporates these into his own verse renditions. In pondering how to mold Anglo-Saxon style in modern forms, he discovers new force in both the style of Anglo-Saxon verse itself and in the capacity of modern English to express it. Greenfield's is an interesting and successful experiment; he provides access to this ancient style more by way of a recreation than by historical placement. In Roy F. Leslie's essay we see the editor at work, using, once again, the stylistic criteria already described to solve, or propose solutions for, some of the persistent cruces in the Old English elegies. Leslie's suggestion that stylistic questions should be given weight in editorial decisions goes far beyond the attitudes of nineteenth-century scholars; his method will stimulate a considered re-evaluation of the editing process.

As this introduction reveals, much of the study of style in Old English poetry has centered on repetition, particularly that repetition called variation. The study has rarely been sympathetic; it has most often applied esthetic standards which did not show the poetry in its best light. Fred C. Robinson here treats both these items and their relation in detail; he articulates an expanded definition of variation and gives us solid reasons for appreciating repetition as a literary device. Finally, Peter Clemoes probes another question of style through focusing on Anglo-Saxon descriptive technique and the way of knowing that this implies. He identifies an indivisible relationship between action and the doer of it as the primary concern of Old English poetry and considers how this mode of perception structures the narrative and controls the meaning of *Beowulf*.

The variety contained in these essays implies that no individual method or viewpoint will account for every facet of Anglo-Saxon verbal art. But each broadens the area of its special concern and collectively the essays push wide the boundaries of the field. For they share a common interest in language, meaning, and the part that all stylistic effects play in fusing the word and the idea.

Works Cited

Adams, Eleanor N. *Old English Scholarship in England from 1566–1800*. New Haven 1917.

Andrew, Samuel O. *Postscript on Beowulf*. New York 1948; repr. 1969.

———. *Syntax and Style in Old English*. Cambridge 1940.

Bartlett, Adeline C. *The Larger Rhetorical Patterns in Anglo-Saxon Poetry.* New York 1935.

Beaty, John O. "The Echo-Word in *Beowulf* with a Note on the *Finnsburg Fragment,*" *PMLA* 49 (1934) 365-73.

Binns, A. L. "'Linguistic' Reading: Two Suggestions of the Quality of Literature," *Essays on Style and Language: Linguistic and Critical Approaches to Literary Style,* ed. Roger Fowler. London 1966. Pp. 118-34.

Bode, William. *Die Kenningar in der angelsächsischen Dichtung.* Darmstadt 1886.

Bone, Gavin. *Anglo-Saxon Poetry: An Essay, with Specimen Translations in Verse.* Oxford 1943.

Bosworth, Joseph. *The Elements of Anglo-Saxon Grammar.* London 1823.

Brandl, Alois. *Englische Literatur: A. Angelsächsische Periode,* Hermann Paul's *Grundriss der germanischen Philologie* vol. 2 pt. 1. 2nd ed. Strasbourg 1901-09. Pp. 941-1134.

Bright, James W., ed. *An Anglo-Saxon Reader.* New York 1891.

Brink, Bernhard A. K. ten. *History of English Literature,* trans. Horace M. Kennedy. 2 vols. in 3 New York 1883-96.

Brodeur, Arthur G. *The Art of Beowulf.* Berkeley 1959.

———. "A Study of Diction and Style in Three Anglo-Saxon Narrative Poems," *Nordica et Anglica: Studies in Honor of Stefán Einarrson,* ed. Allan H. Orrick. The Hague 1968. Pp. 13-26.

Brooke, Stopford A. *The History of Early English Literature.* New York and London 1892.

Burchfield, Robert W. "The Prosodic Terminology of Anglo-Saxon Scholars," *Old English Studies in Honour of John C. Pope,* ed. Robert B. Burlin and Edward B. Irving, Jr. Toronto 1974. Pp. 171-202.

Burlin, Robert B. *The Old English 'Advent': A Typological Commentary.* New Haven 1968.

Campbell, A. "The Old English Epic Style," *English and Medieval Studies Presented to J. R. R. Tolkien on the Occasion of his Seventieth Birthday,* ed. Norman Davis and C. L. Wrenn. London 1962. Pp. 13-26.

Campbell, Jackson J. "Knowledge of Rhetorical Figures in Anglo-Saxon England," *Journal of English and Germanic Philology* 66 (1967) 1-20.

———. "Learned Rhetoric in Old English Poetry," *Modern Philology* 63 (1966) 189-201.

Chambers, Raymond W., ed. *Widsith: A Study in Old English Heroic Legend.* Cambridge 1912.

Clemoes, Peter. *Rhythm and Cosmic Order in Old English Christian Literature.* Cambridge 1970.

Conner, Patrick W. "Schematization of Oral-Formulaic Processes in Old English Poetry," *Language and Style* 5 (1972) 204–20.

Conybeare, John J. *Illustrations of Anglo-Saxon Poetry*, ed. William D. Conybeare. London 1826.

Courthope, William J. *A History of English Poetry.* 6 vols. London 1820–26. Vol. 1.

Creed, Robert P. "On the Possibility of Criticizing Old English Poetry," *Texas Studies in Literature and Language* 3 (1961) 97–106.

Deutschbein, Max. *Zur Entwicklung des englischen Alliterationsverses.* Halle 1902.

Ellis, George. *Specimens of the Early English Poets.* 3 vols. London 1801. Vol. 1.

Fakundiny, Lydia. "The Art of Old English Verse Composition, Part II," *Review of English Studies* ser. 2, 21 (1970) 257–66.

Foster, T. Gregory. *Judith: Studies in Metre, Language and Style,* Quellen und Forschungen 71. Strasbourg 1892.

Fox, Samuel, ed. *Menologium seu Calendarium Poeticum.* London 1830.

Frank, Roberta. "Some Uses of Paronomasia in Old English Scriptural Verse," *Speculum* 47 (1972) 207–26.

Gaebler, Hermann. "Ueber die Autorschaft des angelsaechsischen Gedichtes vom Phoenix," *Anglia* 3 (1880) 488–526.

Götzinger, Ernst. *Ueber die Dichtungen des Angelsachsen Caedmon und deren Verfasser.* Göttingen 1860.

Gradon, Pamela. *Form and Style in Early English Literature.* London 1971.

Greenfield, Stanley B. *The Interpretation of Old English Poems.* London and Boston 1972.

Grimm, Jakob, ed. *Andreas und Elene.* Cassel 1840.

Guest, Edwin. *A History of English Rhythms.* 2 vols. London 1838. Vol. 1.

Gummere, Francis B. *The Anglo-Saxon Metaphor.* Halle 1881.

Haarder, Andreas. *Beowulf: The Appeal of a Poem.* Aarhus 1975.

Hawkes, Terence. *Metaphor.* London 1972.

Heinzel, Richard. *Über den Stil der altgermanischen Poesie*, Quellen und Forschungen 10. Strasbourg 1875.

Heusler, Andreas. "Der Dialog in der altgermanischen erzählenden Dichtung," *Zeitschrift für deutsches Alterthum* 46 (1902) 189-284.

_____. "Heliand, Liedstil und Epenstil," *Zeitschrift für deutsches Alterthum* 57 (1920) 1-48.

Hickes, George. *Grammatica Anglo-Saxonica.* Oxford 1711; repr. Scolar Press 1970.

_____. *Linguarum Vett. Septentrionalium Thesaurus Grammatico-Criticus et Archaeologicus.* 2 vols. Oxford 1705. Vol. 1.

Hoffmann, A. "Der bildliche Ausdruck in *Beówulf* und in der Edda," *Englische Studien* 6 (1883) 163-216.

Hoffmann, Otto. *Reimformeln im Westgermanischen.* Darmstadt 1885.

Huppé, Bernard F. *The Web of Words; Structural Analyses of the Old English Poems: Vainglory; The Wonder of Creation; The Dream of the Rood; and Judith.* Albany 1970.

Johnson, Samuel. *A Dictionary of the English Language.* 2 vols. London 1755. Vol. 1.

Kail, J. "Über die Parallelstellen in der angelsächsischen Poesie," *Anglia* 12 (1889) 21-40.

Kapp, Volker. "Das Stil-Konzept in den Anfängen der romanistischen Stilforschung," *In Memoriam Friedrich Diez: Akten des Kolloquiums zur Wissenschaftsgeschichte der Romanistik,* ed. Hans-Josef Niederehe and Harald Haarman, Amsterdam Studies in the Theory and History of Linguistic Science ser. 3 vol. 9. Amsterdam 1976.

Kemble, John M. "Letter to M. Francisque Michel," Francisque Michel, *Bibliothèque Anglo-Saxonne.* Paris and London 1837. Pp. 12-13.

_____. *The Poetry of the Codex Vercellensis, with an English Translation,* Aelfric Society 5-6. 2 vols. in 1 London 1843-56.

Ker, William P. *Epic and Romance: Essays on Medieval Literature.* London and New York 1897.

Kershaw, Nora, ed. and trans. *Anglo-Saxon and Norse Poems.* Cambridge 1922.

Kintgen, Eugene R. "Echoic Repetition in Old English Poetry, Especially *The Dream of the Rood,*" *Neuphilologische Mitteilungen* 75 (1974) 202-23.

Köhler, Artur. "Über den Stand berufsmässiger Sänger in nationalen Epos germanischer Völker," *Germania* 15 (1870) 27-50.

Körting, Gustav. *Grundriss der Geschichte der englischen Literatur.* Münster 1887.

62   *Daniel G. Calder*

Krapp, George Philip. "The Parenthetic Exclamation in Old English Poetry," *Modern Language Notes* 20 (1905) 33–37.

Laborde, E. D. "The Style of *The Battle of Maldon*," *Modern Language Review* 19 (1924) 401–17.

Lawrence, William W. "Structure and Interpretation of *Widsith*," *Modern Philology* 4 (1906) 329–74.

Leslie, Roy F. "Analysis of Stylistic Devices and Effects in Anglo-Saxon Literature," *Stil- und Formprobleme in der Literatur*, ed. Paul Böckmann, 7th Congress of the International Federation for Modern Languages and Literatures. Heidelberg 1959. Pp. 129–36.

Leyerle, John. "The Interlace Structure of *Beowulf*," *University of Toronto Quarterly* 37 (1967/8) 1–17.

Longfellow, Henry Wadsworth. "Anglo-Saxon Literature," *North American Review* 47 (1839) 90–134.

Lord, Albert B. *The Singer of Tales*. Cambridge Mass. 1960.

Magoun, Francis P., Jr. "*Béowulf Á:* A Folk-Variant," *Arv* 14 (1958) 95–101.

————. "*Béowulf B:* A Folk-Poem on Béowulf's Death," *Early English and Norse Studies, Presented to Hugh Smith in Honour of his Sixtieth Birthday*, ed. Arthur Brown and Peter Foote. London 1963. Pp. 127–40.

————. "Oral-Formulaic Character of Anglo-Saxon Narrative Poetry," *Speculum* 28 (1953) 446–63.

————. "Some Notes on Anglo-Saxon Poetry," *Studies in Medieval Literature in Honor of Professor Albert Croll Baugh*, ed. MacEdward Leach. Philadelphia 1961. Pp. 273–83.

Malone, Kemp. "Plurilinear Units in Old English Poetry," *Review of English Studies* 19 (1943) 201–04.

————, ed. *Widsith*. London 1936.

Marquardt, Hertha. *Die altenglischen Kennigar: Ein Beitrag zur Stilkunde altgermanischer Dichtung*, Schriften der Königsberger Gelehrten Gesellschaft 14 no. 3, Geisteswissenschaftliche Klasse. Halle 1938. Pp. 103–340.

Merbot, Reinhold. *Ästhetische Studien zur angelsächsischen Poesie*. Breslau 1883.

Merwe Scholtz, Hendrik van der. *The Kenning in Anglo-Saxon and Old Norse Poetry*. Oxford 1929.

Meyer, Richard M. *Die altgermanische Poesie nach ihren formelhaften Elementen beschrieben*. Berlin 1889.

Müllenhoff, Karl. "Die innere Geschichte des *Beovulfs*," *Zeitschrift für deutsches Alterthum* 14 (1869) 193–244.

Ohmann, Richard. "Generative Grammars and the Concept of Literary Style," *Word* 20 (1964) 423-39.

Paetzel, Walther. *Die Variationen in der altgermanischen Allitterationspoesie*, Palaestra 48. Berlin 1913.

Percy, Thomas. *Reliques of Ancient Poetry*. 3 vols. London 1765. Vol. 2.

Petheram, John. *An Historical Sketch of the Progress and Present State of Anglo-Saxon Literature in England*. London 1840.

Price, Richard, ed. Thomas Warton's *The History of English Poetry, from the Close of the Eleventh to the Commencement of the Eighteenth Century*. 2nd ed. 4 vols. London 1824.

Quirk, Randolph. "Poetic Language and Old English Metre," *Essays on the English Language: Medieval and Modern*. Bloomington Ind. 1968. Pp. 1-19.

Rask, Rasmus K. *A Grammar of the Anglo-Saxon Tongue, with a Praxis*, new ed. trans. Benjamin Thorpe. Copenhagen 1830.

Renoir, Alain. "*Judith* and the Limits of Poetry," *English Studies* 43 (1962) 145-55.

Richards, I. A. *The Philosophy of Rhetoric*. London and New York 1936.

Robinson, Fred C. "Lexicography and Literary Criticism: A Caveat," *Philological Essays: Studies in Old and Middle English Language and Literature, in Honour of Herbert Dean Meritt*, ed. James L. Rosier. The Hague 1970. Pp. 99-110.

_____. "The Significance of Names in Old English Literature," *Anglia* 86 (1968) 14-58.

_____. "Some Uses of Name-Meanings in Old English Poetry," *Neuphilologische Mitteilungen* 69 (1968) 161-71.

_____. "Variation: A Study in the Diction of *Beowulf*," unpublished Ph.D. Dissertation, University of North Carolina 1961.

Rosier, James L. "The Literal-Figurative Identity of The *Wanderer*," *PMLA* 79 (1964) 366-69.

Rynell, Alarik. *Parataxis and Hypotaxis as a Criterion of Syntax and Style, Especially in Old English Poetry*. Lund 1952.

Sarrazin, G. "Die 'Fata Apostolorum' und der Dichter Kynewulf," *Anglia* 12 (1889) 375-87.

_____. "Parallelstellen in altenglischer Dichtung," *Anglia* 14 (1892) 186-92.

Schaar, Claes. *Critical Studies in the Cynewulf Group*. Lund 1949.

Schemann, Karl F. *Die Synonyma im Beowulfsliede mit Rücksicht auf Composition und Poetik des Gedichtes*. Hagen 1882.

Schroeder, Peter R. "Stylistic Analogies between Old English Art and Poetry," *Viator* 5 (1974) 185-97.

Schwarz, Franz H. A. *Cynewulfs Anteil am Christ.* Königsberg 1905.

Shelton, Maurice, trans. *Wotton's Short View of George Hickes's Grammatico-Critical and Archeological Treasure of the Ancient Northern Languages.* London 1735.

Shibles, Warren A., comp. *Essays on Metaphor.* Whitewater Wisc. 1972.

Shippey, T. A. *Old English Verse.* London 1972.

Sievers, Eduard. *Der Heliand und die angelsächsische Genesis.* Halle 1875.

Stanley, E. G. "Old English Poetic Diction and the Interpretation of *The Wanderer, The Seafarer,* and *The Penitent's Prayer,*" *Anglia* 73 (1956) 413-66.

Storms, Godfrid. "The Subjectivity of the Style of *Beowulf,*" *Studies in Old English Literature, in Honor of Arthur G. Brodeur,* ed. Stanley B. Greenfield. Eugene Ore. 1963. Pp. 171-86.

Sweet, Henry. "Sketch of the History of Anglo-Saxon Poetry," Thomas Warton's *History of English Poetry from the Twelfth to the Close of the Sixteenth Century,* ed. W. Carew Hazlitt. 4th ed. 4 vols. London 1871. Vol. 2 pp. 1-19.

Taine, Hippolyte. *History of English Literature,* trans. Henri van Laun. New York 1873.

Thorpe, Benjamin. *Analecta Anglo-Saxonica.* 2nd ed. London 1868.

_____, ed. *Caedmon's Metrical Paraphrase of Parts of the Holy Scriptures, in Anglo-Saxon.* London 1832.

Tolkien, J. R. R. "Beowulf: The Monsters and the Critics," *Proceedings of the British Academy* 22 (1936) 245-95.

Tolman, Albert H. "The Style of Anglo-Saxon Poetry," *PMLA* 3 (1887) 17-47.

Turner, Sharon. *The History of the Anglo-Saxons from the Earliest Period to the Norman Conquest.* 5th ed. 3 vols. London 1828. Vol. 3.

Tyrwhitt, Thomas, ed. *The Canterbury Tales of Chaucer.* 5 vols. London 1775-78. Vol. 4.

Warton, Thomas. *The History of English Poetry, from the Close of the Eleventh to the Commencement of the Eighteenth Century.* 3 vols. London 1774-81. Vol. 1.

Wheelwright, Philip E. *Metaphor and Reality.* Bloomington Ind. 1962.

Wolff, Ludwig, "Über den Stil der altgermanischen Poesie," *Deutsches Vierteljahrschrift* 1 (1923) 214-29.

Woolf, Rosemary. "Doctrinal Influences on *The Dream of the Rood*," *Medium Aevum* 27 (1958) 137-53.

Wright, Thomas. "Introductory Essay on the State of Literature and Learning under the Anglo-Saxons," *Biographia Britannica Literaria*. 2 vols. London 1842-46. Vol. 1 pp. 1-112.

Wyld, Henry Cecil. "Diction and Imagery in Anglo-Saxon Poetry," *Essays and Studies* 11 (1925) 49-91.

Ziegler, Heinrich. *Der poetische Sprachgebrauch in der sogen. Caedmonschen Dichtungen*. Münster 1883.

TWO OLD ENGLISH POETIC PHRASES INSUFFICIENTLY UNDERSTOOD FOR LITERARY CRITICISM: *ÞING GEHEGAN* AND *SEONOÞ GEHEGAN*

E. G. Stanley

TWO PASSAGES of Old English verse will be discussed in this paper, *Beowulf* 419-26 and *Phoenix* 491-94. Usually, when one undertakes the discussion of a passage or two of Old English verse, the hope is to contribute elucidation. In fact, obfuscation is not infrequently an unintentional result; the following discussion differs from such in obfuscating intentionally. After a century and a half of serious and informed *Beowulf* scholarship we have our orthodoxies of understanding and may even feel safe enough for literary criticism of points of detail requiring a familiarity with the overtones of the original which, I believe, we lack. The study of the other long poems is less well developed, and the notes and commentaries on them are less full. Even so, for them too literary interpretations are advanced with hope of success, which would be courage if the exercise were dangerous. I wish to test the ice at two places; at one of them we have for a long time executed our more daring figurative skating, though I expect to find the ice thin; and the other place is similar to it, but less frequented.

First, *Beowulf* 419-26:

selfe ofersawon,　ða ic of searwum cwom,
fah from feondum,　þær ic fife geband,
yðde eotena cyn,　ond on yðum slog
niceras nihtes,　nearoþearfe dreah,
wræc Wedera nið　—wean ahsodon—,
forgrand gramum;　ond nu wið Grendel sceal,
wið þam aglæcan　ana gehegan
ðing wið þyrse.[1]

The text is that of Klaeber's great edition, and his magnificent notes are used by me of course. Here in Beowulf's speech vowing to take on Grendel, though there are some prevailing orthodoxies, Klaeber's notes make it clear that we do not understand the whole of the background. They also make clear, as do Hoops's in his *Kommentar* and Dobbie's in *The Anglo-Saxon Poetic Records*, that the interpretation of some of the wording is disputed. The subject of this paper is chiefly *gehegan ðing* near the end of the passage. Because I wish to show the insecurity of our understanding of the words of complex poetry, using that phrase merely as one example, I point out the obscurities of the context, which I regard as typical in difficulty for the poem as a whole. Hoops and Dobbie admonish us to interpret *of searwum* (419) with Kock as 'from insidious fights' and to have no truck with those who, simple souls, think our hero was taking off his uncomfortable mail-shirt, though that is the most common meaning of *searo* 'contrivance' in the poem. Two etymologically distinct words have the form *fah* in *Beowulf*. It can be the word meaning 'stained'; if we had been allowed to think of Beowulf taking off his mail-shirt we might have thought that *fah* could have referred to the iron or even rust marks where it rubbed his skin or, if they wore such things and did not regard them as beneath epic dignity, his underwear; other interpreters, Heyne for example,

---

1. 'They themselves looked on when I came from insidious fights (*or perhaps* took off my skillfully wrought armor), hostile (*or perhaps* rust- *or* blood-stained) from the enemies, where I bound five, destroyed a race of giants, and in the waves struck down water-monsters in the night, endured rigorous distress, avenged the Weder-Geats' strife—they had asked for woe (*or* courted trouble)—, crushed to death the foes; and now I alone must hold parley (*or* settle the dispute) with Grendel, that fierce one, that monster'.

have thought of him more gloriously as 'blood-stained'. Again
Hoops is sure that *fah* is the other word, 'hostile', and not both
at once, though Klaeber in his first two editions gave 'blood-
stained' with a question mark in his glossaries, and in his third
gives the line reference under both words, both times with a
question mark. That seems best for Beowulf coming from the
fight, for our poet used both senses at once happily combined
for Cain (1263), hostile and bearing his mark, therefore
'marked', the ambiguity of a single word summing up a great
deal of Genesis 4:11-15.

Part of the obscurity of the poem as far as a literary understanding is concerned is that we do not know what criteria to
adopt for visualizing monsters. In the passage under discussion we have three kinds, the *eotena cyn* (421) five of which
Beowulf bound before he, *fah*, disengaged himself *of searwum*, the *niceras* he slew by night, and Grendel described as
an *aglæca* and a *þyrs*. What size was an *eoten* is no mere fresh-
men's question to be dismissed, as Dr. Faustus does a different form of computational skill; for we wish to know
whether Grendel was no bigger than, for example, Jutes might
seem in one persuasive interpretation of the confusion in our
poem of the forms for Jutes and giants (as a result of which the
eotena bearn [1088] of the Finnsburg Episode are one *eotena
cyn*).[2] If the Jutes were thought gigantic, then the giants need
not have been thought very monstrously tall, but tall enough to

2. Cf. lines 883, 1088, 1141; see Robert E. Kaske, "The *Eotenas* in *Beowulf*," in *Old English Poetry: Fifteen Essays*, ed. Robert P. Creed (Provi-
dence R.I. 1967) 285-310. For references to occurrences in Old English of
the various words for monsters, etc., and earlier scholarship, see, in addition
to the information given in Klaeber's edition, Richard Jente, *Die mytholo-
gischen Ausdrücke im altenglischen Wortschatz*, Anglistische Forschungen
56 (Heidelberg 1921); for *eoten*, 184-85 (the first suggestion that the word is
related to the name of the Jutes is to be found in Jacob Grimm, *Deutsche
Mythologie* [Göttingen 1835] 296-97 [cf. Jente, 185 n. 2]); for *þyrs*, 187-89;
for *nicor*, 140-41. For *þyrs*, see further, Jan de Vries, *Altnordisches etymologisches Wörterbuch* (Leiden 1962) s.v. *þurs*, especially for the Finno-Ugrian
etymologies. For Higlacus' size, see Dorothy Whitelock, *The Audience of
Beowulf* (Oxford 1951) 46. Professor Fred C. Robinson, who kindly read the
typescript and made valuable comments on several points, rightly suggests
that I should draw attention to the fact that the Haupt Gloss for *þyrs* is

overtop a Geat who is likely to have been taller than his maternal uncle King Higlacus, described in the *Liber Monstrorum* as of such size that from his twelfth year no horse could carry him, his bones still preserved centuries later and shown to travelers from afar as a miracle. Such a man must have been nearer in size to those "etayns" compared with whom the huge Green Knight of *Sir Gawain and the Green Knight* was half at most, the poet supposes, for he was small enough to be carried by a *hors gret and þikke*—but it would be rash to assume that the size of the individuals that constituted the *eotena cyn* destroyed by Beowulf in a battle mentioned in passing was identical with that of the *etaynez* with whom the *Gawain* poet (723) makes his hero fight in a battle mentioned even more casually, for the space of time separating the two poets is greater than the space of time that separates us from the *Gawain* poet, more than long enough for a nation to lose all continuity in its sense of monstrous proportions. The nature of a *þyrs* has been discussed without success; in English usage he appears to have his dwelling, both in *Beowulf* and in the Cotton *Maxims* (42), in the marshlands; the word (slightly emended) translates Aldhelm's 'cyclopes' in *Riddle* 40 (63)—singled out, admittedly, for their voracity without mention that they are monocule. The Corpus Glossary (1457) like the much later Cleopatra Glosses (WW, 459, 31) make the word the equivalent of *orcus*, but the latter have it (WW, 378, 25; 379, 22) for *cyclops* too, and once for Cacus (WW, 376, 19), if it really is the three-headed son of Vulcan as the editor, R. P. Wülcker, thinks. Other meanings in the glossaries are even less like what we might imagine Grendel to be in appearance, though the equivalence of him with *heldiobul* (Corpus, alternative gloss at 1457) gives his spiritual nature, distantly supported by Notker's comment on Psalm 17:32 that the gods of the heathen are *daemonia*, 'little spirits', for which he cites

---

incomplete: cf. Louis Goossens, *The Old English Glosses of MS. Brussels, Royal Library, 1650 (Aldhelm's de Laudibus Virginitatis)*, Verhandelingen van de Koninklijke Academie voor Wetenschappen, Letteren en Schone Kunsten van België, Klasse der Letteren 36 no. 74 (Brussels 1974) 253 No. 1637.

the Old High German *tursa* (nominative plural), the only occurrence of the cognate in that language. That sounds less imposing than the lemma *colossi* of the Haupt Glosses (445, 2; compare the edition by Louis Goossens [1974], *þyr* [No. 1637]) and their parallel in the Napier Glosses (1637), as well as the gigantic *þurs* of Old Norse who seems to have given his name to a sea-monster in evidence among Baltic peoples dwelling east of the Scandinavian tribes. The resources at our disposal, namely the context in which the word is found, the testimony of the lemmata to which it provides an explanation for the Anglo-Saxons (at times together with an alternative gloss), and the evidence of continental and Scandinavian cognates and the loanwords derived from the last, shed no light on that creature of darkness, though there is nothing to contradict what we know about the *þyrs* Grendel from our poem, that he was larger than an ordinary Dane or Geat, and that he was at home under water. We may add to that that he was of the devil's kind. The etymology of the word is obscure. As we read Hoops's *Kommentar* on *niceras* (422) we get what is, I think, a false impression that we can feel the ground under our feet. He says that the word is probably the general term for strange larger aquatic beasts, both real and fabulous, and he gives the sense 'water-monster' for the word. The distinction between real and fabulous is, however, ours and not demonstrably that of the Anglo-Saxons. We know that there are no sirens, no mermaids or mermen, though their existence may have been believed in by the Anglo-Saxons. At the same time we really believe, and know that we are right to believe, in the existence of the hippopotamus which *nicor* translates several times in "The Letter of Alexander the Great", as Bosworth-Toller plus *Supplement* and *Enlarged Addenda* make clear. In the Old High German Glosses the cognate *nihhus* several times translates crocodile, and we know all about crocodiles. The Icelandic cognate, *nykr*, also stands for hippopotamus, though more often for a fabulous being of the sea, like those in *Beowulf* perhaps. There appears to be general agreement on the etymology, with or without *-r* suffix. What we do not know is how the Anglo-Saxons imagined a *nicor*, perhaps like a

horse as has been suggested for the common Germanic concept, perhaps like some other monster, for not many of them
will have seen hippopotamuses or crocodiles, not many more
than had seen sirens or mermen. "It is not clear," says Klaeber in his note on lines 420-24, "whether these feats were performed in the course of a single adventure or on several occa-
sions"; he wonders whether perhaps the slaying of these
niceras by night could refer to the Breca episode where (575)
nine *niceras* were slain, it seems at night too. He adds, "the
definite sense of 'walrus,' 'hippopotamus' . . . need not be
looked for in the *Beowulf*". He is, however, sure—as is Hoops
in his note on line 423—that *niceras* is the subject of *ahsodon*.
No wonder we are not to look for some zoologically real sense
in *niceras*, for in modern experience the hippopotamus and
the crocodile never ask for woe. If the *niceras* were able to
speak they must have been more like mermen or mermaids.

Two things, however, are far from certain: first, the literal
or non-literal nature of the phrase *wean ahsodon*; and secondly, the tight or looser syntax of the passage as a result of which
we may be able to say who did the asking. First, the phrase: it
occurs also at line 1206, where Hygelac is said to ask for woe of
the Frisians, and *wean* 'woe' is varied by and in grammatical
apposition to *fæhðe* 'enmity' the former combination being a
metaphor different in flavor, 'to ask for trouble' which he
found in the shape of death, different from the latter, 'to seek
enmity', where 'to ask' is not quite literal but lacks the grim
irony of *wean ahsode*:

> Ðone hring hæfde   Higelac Geata,
> nefa Swertinges   nyhstan siðe,
> siðþan he under segne   sinc ealgode,
> wælreaf werede;   hyne wyrd fornam,
> syþðan he for wlenco   wean ahsode,
> fæhðe to Frysum.[3]   (1202-07)

We cannot tell how the rhetorical parallelism of the two clauses

3. 'Hygelac of the Geats had that ring [the one given by Hrothgar to Beowulf, and alone fit for comparison with the Brisinga men] for the last time,
when he, the descendant of Swerting, under the standard defended the treasure, protected the booty of war; destiny destroyed him when he in his pride
asked for woe, for enmity at the hands of the Frisians'.

introduced by *siðþan* (*syþðan*) relates to the underlying sense, whether the defense of the treasure is somehow to be regarded as in itself a prideful asking for woe, and we are not told if the treasure here defended is simply the great ring with which the sentence opens—as I think it must be—and, if so, how it acquired the seemingly blood-stained description *wælreaf*, literally 'slaughter-booty'. We sense the irony in the phrase *wean ahsode*, which, as we know for a fact, is a non-literal phrase, but we do not know what the irony consists in, because we are not told by the poet in an allusive context characteristic of him, as he moves forward to the concluding phrase, still metaphorically dependent on *ahsode*, but without the irony of *wean ahsode*, 'he asked for enmity at the hands of the Frisians'.

In dealing with an ancient text one ought to ask oneself at every point where an interpretation is attempted, and in answering try to assess how far an answer is possible in view of our limited knowledge and understanding of what they knew and understood, how does our understanding differ from theirs? The phrase *wean ahsode* clearly exemplifies change in understanding, recent change. I am not so much concerned with the gain in grammatical knowledge for which we are indebted chiefly to the articles by Klaeber (they are referred to by him in his glossary, s.v. *āhsian*, and also by Hoops in his note on line 423), that without the prefix *ge-* the verb *ahsian* cannot have the sense 'find out' and therefore 'experience'; but rather with the development in recent English, not recorded in *OED, Second Supplement*, s.v. *ask*, 16.b., before the twentieth century, of such phrases as *to ask for trouble*, or more colloquially *he asked for it and he got it*. Inevitably, our understanding is colored by that recent usage. There can be no question of continuity with the Old English ironic phrase, but it recreates for us an ironic habit of understanding into which to fit the two uses in *Beowulf*, even though the solemn tone of the Old English poem is far distant from the flippancy of the twentieth-century usage.

Though the exact significance of the parallelism, *siðþan . . . syþðan . . .*, of lines 1204 ff. is not to be determined and may not have been thought of as an exact significance by the poet, our understanding of the context of that use of *wean ahsode* is

clear in comparison with our understanding of the context of
the phrase at line 423. It seems doubtful to me if Hoops's
certainty, that the subject of *wean ahsodon* is *niceras*, is conclusive. The mere fact that Klaeber's text has dashes surrounding the phrase indicates that there is some discontinuity
in construction; Klaeber follows the punctuation of Heyne
(first in 1863, and still in Else von Schaubert's revisions),
where Grein (first in 1857) follows editions, like Thorpe's
translation, with parentheses. None of the editors of the poem
seems to punctuate the passage without resorting to one or
other of these marks of discontinuity. Klaeber's doubts
whether the feats described in lines 420–24 were performed by
Beowulf in the course of a single adventure or on several occa-
sions should make us pause before we accept, as he does,
niceras as the subject of *ahsodon*, and should incline us to the
possibility at least—in *Beowulf* certainties of how syntactic
structures hang together are not always easy to come by—that
the subject of *ahsodon* may well be those who or which brought
about *Wedera nið*, the enemies, five of them, a race of giants,
those hostile ones whose crushing is described in the phrase
forgrand gramum (424). That looser interpretation of the passage receives no support, however, from any of the other short
parenthetical clauses marked off as such by the editors of the
poem. Ultimately it rests only on an impression gained from
the poet's use of the general terms *feondum* and *gramum* (a
dative plural forming part of a different structure) to surround
the specific *eotena cyn* and *niceras*, as well as his use of the
general *Wedera nið* immediately preceding *wean ahsodon*.

Some of the sound-effects of the poem, whether intentional
wordplay or the chance result of the essential use of alliteration, can be assessed by us only impressionistically. At one
place in our passage, line 421, the texture has become more
paronomastic, and therefore richer, with the passage of time
and change of dialect from what was presumably an Anglian
original, perhaps of the later eighth century or rather earlier
or, as I think is more probable, later even, to the text as it
survives in a roughly West-Saxon manuscript of about 1000.
As the text stands, *ȳðe* / *ȳðum* looks like wordplay; there may

have been some inexact jingle in an original *ēðdæ / ȳðum* or slightly better in early West-Saxon *īeðdæ / ȳðum* (not that it is at all likely that the poem was written in early West-Saxon), but the original vowel of the stem-syllable of the verb is not echoed exactly in the noun of the original. On the other hand, across a heavy mark of punctuation at the caesura of the line (424) the stem of *forgrand* seems close in sound to that of Grendel. Perhaps we are to feel that Beowulf, the man of whom it is said that he crushed to destruction those enemies whose defeat we have heard about so far, will be the right hero to take on Grendel: that sounds right paronomastically, and has more substantial support if it is true that *Grendel* and *grindan* are etymologically related,[4] though of course it is not in the nature of things that the Anglo-Saxons themselves should have been able to distinguish etymology from word-play, or would have thought of making that distinction.

Grendel is described as an *aglæca*, a word which we do not understand. One scholar has, in fact, made investigation of this word a model for the methodology of establishing meaning.[5] The attempt is of interest, but in the end we always come back to the fact that, as Klaeber's glossary shows, the word is used by the poet not only to describe Grendel as here, and later in the poem to describe the dragon, and the monsters of the mere as they attack Beowulf, but also Beowulf himself; and at one point the two enemies, Beowulf and the dragon, are described together by the plural *aglæcean*. As we assemble the many uses including compounds and including a use in prose, as we look at the cognates and at the Middle English derivative *egleche*, it becomes clear only that it is not pejorative in force.

4. To the etymologies given by Klaeber, xxviii–xxix, add A. H. Smith, *English Place-Name Elements* 1, English Place-Name Society 25 (Cambridge 1956) 209.

5. Doreen M. E. Gillam, "The Use of the Term 'aeglaeca' in *Beowulf* at Lines 893 and 2592," *Studia Germanica Gandensia* 3 (1961) 145–69; Miss Gillam uses the word again as an example within a discussion of the wider issue of "A Method for Determining the Connotations of O.E. Poetic Words," *Studia Germanica Gandensia* 6 (1964) 85–101. For an etymology, cf. Claude M. Lotspeich, "Old English Etymologies," *Journal of English and Germanic Philology* 40 (1941) 1.

We must not follow Klaeber's distinction of 'wretch, monster, demon, fiend' for Beowulf's enemies, and 'warrior, hero' for Beowulf himself; and we must not abuse Grendel's mother when she is called *aglæcwif* by translating the word as Klaeber does, 'wretch', or 'monster, of a woman'. We must never forget that she is called there *ides aglæcwif* (1259), and *ides*, 'lady', is not a term of abuse. Once again, and hard for us to accept when we hope to have formed some picture of the figures of the poem such as is a prerequisite for literary criticism, we may have to recognize that the poet does not speak of his monsters abusively: one of the two had the likeness of a lady (*idese onlicnes*) and Grendel himself was of the stature of a man (*on weres wæstmum*; 1351-52).

Now at last we are ready for *gehegan ðing*. As we have seen, the context is too obscure for us to be able to be sure of what is a plain statement and what is ironic; if only we knew how the Anglo-Saxons themselves looked upon Grendel. We cannot even be quite sure if the phrase is used figuratively. We are not sure of the etymology of *gehegan*, though the current view is to be accepted, alas. The earlier etymology was more picturesque. It used to be thought that *-hegan* means 'to hedge about'. Heyne's edition (1863) is explicit: "*hegen, umzäunen*; þing gehegan *die Gerichtsstätte abstecken, Gericht halten*; hier bildlich."[6] The current etymology leads simply to the sense 'perform, carry out, achieve', and with words meaning 'meeting', like Old English *þing* or *seonoþ*, the verb means 'hold (a meeting)'.[7] It is just as well that we have surrendered a picturesque etymology for one that evokes no scene perhaps to be

6. See Moritz Heyne, *Beovulf* (Paderborn 1863) 192. For the beginning of this etymology, see Jacob Grimm, *Deutsche Grammatik* (Göttingen 1819-37; second edition of vol. 1 [1822]) 416; and still in Jacob and Wilhelm Grimm, *Deutsches Wörterbuch*, ed. Moritz Heyne 4.2 (Leipzig 1877) 777-78, s.v. *hegen*, as well as in Alfred Götze, *Trübners Deutsches Wörterbuch* 3 (Berlin 1939) 376-77, s.v.; and perhaps also (at least by implication) in K. A. Eckhardt's fourth edition of Karl von Amira, *Germanisches Recht* [in Hermann Paul's *Grundriss der germanischen Philologie* 5.2] 2 (Berlin 1967) 153-54.

7. See Klaeber's Glossary, s.v.; cf. F. Holthausen, *Altenglisches etymologisches Wörterbuch* (Heidelberg 1934) s.v. *hiegan* 1; Alexander Jóhannes-

connected with the driving in of what the Frisians called the *thingstapul*,[8] with which John Earle almost a hundred years ago connected the *stapol* (926) on which (*on* cannot mean 'by') Hrothgar stood. Even if we believed in the older etymology of *gehegan*, we could hardly have assumed that the Anglo-Saxons would have been conscious of it; and the modern view is, rightly I think, that opaque etymologies determine connotations of words only in the minds of modern scholars, not in the minds of ordinary users of the language.

Klaeber's note is clear on lines 424-26:

> ond nu wið Grendel sceal,
> wið þam aglæcan ana gehegan
> ðing wið þyrse.

He says, "**425 f. gehēgan / ðing**, 'hold a meeting,' 'settle the dispute,' 'fight the case out.' A legal term applied to battle. See Antiq. § 6." At "Antiq. § 6" (p. 272) Klaeber gives the phrase as the first illustration of "Figurative use of **legal** terms (applied to battle, etc.)." The glossary makes clear that the verb *gehegan* is confined to poetry; and that is, of course, confirmed by the dictionaries, from which it emerges that the word is not very rare, that it occurs elsewhere in collocation with *þing* as well as with the loanword *seonoþ* 'synod', and that it has cognates in Old Icelandic and in Old Frisian. The uses in Old English show that the word can be handled either literally or metaphorically. The poet of *Andreas* has a peculiar penchant for *gehegan*. He uses it literally of the convening of a

---

son, *Isländisches etymologisches Wörterbuch* (Bern 1956) 177; Julius Pokorny, *Indogermanisches etymologisches Wörterbuch* 1 (2 vols. Bern 1959-69) 950; Jan de Vries (n. 2 above) s.v. *heyja*.

8. See B. E. Siebs, *Grundlagen und Aufbau der altfriesischen Verfassung*, Untersuchungen zur Deutschen Staats- und Rechtsgeschichte 144 (Breslau 1933) 89-90: the ceremonies described by Siebs as the magical marking off of the place where the thing is held are those connected with the older etymology of Old Frisian *heia*; Siebs's *Gerichtspfahl* is the *thingstapul*. For the suggested connection between that word and *Beowulf* 926, see John Earle, *A Hand-Book to the Land-Charters, and other Saxonic Documents* (Oxford 1888) 466-67, and especially Klaeber's note on the line in *Beowulf*; see also A. H. Smith, *English Place-Name Elements* 2, English Place-Name Society 26 (Cambridge 1957) 146.

meeting, *Swa hie symble ymb þritig þing gehedon / nihtgerimes* (157–58), translated and explained by K. R. Brooks, in the standard edition of the poem: " 'Thus they always held a council after thirty nights' . . . Here *þing gehedon* has its literal sense, but *þing gehegan* 930 is simply 'meet'; in 1049 and 1496 *mæðel gehegan* means 'hold speech' or 'converse'. "[9] The same poem has the compound *mæðel-hegende* (variously spelled) three times, either substantively 'one who holds speech' or adjectivally 'holding speech'. I doubt if *þing gehegan* at line 930 simply means 'to meet' as Brooks says (in his note on 157–58), for there too the sense is more like 'attend on an appointed day':

> . . . ðu in Achaia   ondsæc dydest,
> ðæt ðu on feorwegas   feran ne cuðe,
> ne in þa ceastre   becuman mehte,
> þing gehegan   þreora nihta
> fyrstgemearces,   swa ic þe feran het
> ofer wega gewinn.[10]   (*Andreas* 927–32)

An appointed day is not mentioned when the Exeter *Maxims* use *þing . . . gehegan* not far from a more strictly legal phrase, *sace semaþ*:

> Þing sceal gehegan
> frod wiþ frodne;   biþ hyra ferð gelic;
> hi a sace semaþ,   sibbe gelæra ð
> þa ær wonsælge   awegen habbað:
> ræd sceal mid snyttro,   ryht mid wisum,
> til sceal mid tilum.[11]   (*Maxims I* 18–23)

9. K. R. Brooks, ed., *Andreas and The Fates of the Apostles* (Oxford 1961) 68.

10. 'in Achaia you denied that you were able to travel far away nor could arrive at the city, attend at the appointed time of three nights, as I commanded you to travel over the turmoil of waves'.

The phrase *þing gehegan* is not in expansion of the source in such a way that it could be related to a Latin sense in it; for the source at this point, cf. George P. Krapp, ed., *Andreas and The Fates of the Apostles* (Boston 1906) xxv. On the importance, in connection with *þing*, of an appointed time, see Amira-Eckhardt 2 (n. 6 above) 149; and cf. the etymologies in Sigmund Feist, *Vergleichendes Wörterbuch der gotischen Sprache* (Leiden 1939) s.v. *þeihs*, and de Vries (n. 2 above) s.v. *þing*.

11. 'A wise man shall hold a meeting to deal with a wise man; their mind

Nothing in Old English legal texts is faintly like *þing gehegan*, for *gehegan* does not occur outside verse, as we have seen. There are, however, several phrases like *sace seman*: e.g. *saca sehtan* similarly alliterative, and without alliteration *sace (to-)twæman*, all three meaning 'to settle strife'; the phrase *sace seman* itself occurs once in a legal text, namely in the early Kentish Laws of Hlothære and Eadric ostensibly of the later seventh century, though preserved only in the twelfth-century Textus Roffensis.[12] The context of the Kentish legal text is not at all close to that of the phrase in the Exeter *Maxims*, where two gnomic commonplaces seem to be combined. First, that wisdom has its proper place at the *þing*, the meeting, and secondly, the wisdom of peacemaking. The former, as has long been pointed out,[13] has some similarity to the Valkyrie's wise sayings to Sigurthr in *Sigrdrífomál* 24:

> þat ræð ec þér þriðia,   at þú þingi á
>   deilit við heimsca hali;
> þvíat ósviðr maðr   lætr opt qveðin
>   verri orð, enn viti.[14]

---

is alike; they always settle strife, counsel peace which unhappy men had made unavailing (?): good counsel must have concord with wisdom, justice with the wise, good with the good'.

12. See F. Liebermann, *Die Gesetze der Angelsachsen* (3 vols. Halle 1898-1916) 1.10 [Hl 10], and 3.18 § 6; cf. N. R. Ker, *Catalogue of Manuscripts Containing Anglo-Saxon* (Oxford 1957) no. 373. For the other phrases, see Liebermann's *Die Gesetze der Angelsachsen* 2.1 (Wörterbuch) s.vv.

13. See Blanche C. Williams, ed., *Gnomic Poetry in Anglo-Saxon* (New York 1914) 131. "Sigrdrífomál" is probably not early; cf. Jan de Vries, *Altnordische Literaturgeschichte* 1 (in Hermann Paul's *Grundriss der germanischen Philologie* 15 [Berlin 1964]) 88. Proverbial wisdom on not having dealings with fools is common also in later English literature: cf. Bartlett J. Whiting, *Proverbs, Sentences, and Proverbial Phrases* (Cambridge Mass. 1968) F425, F450, S91; cf. *The Owl and the Nightingale* lines 283-306, ed. E. G. Stanley (Manchester 1972) 160-62, as well as, in earlier Icelandic literature, "Hávamál" 122: *orðom skipta þú skalt aldregi / við ósvinna apa*, 'You must never exchange words with a foolish idiot' in a relevant context (cf. *The Hávamál*, ed. Daisy E. Martin Clarke [Cambridge 1923] 74-75).

14. 'Thirdly, I give you this counsel, that at the thing you have no dealings with simpletons; for a silly man does often speak words worse than he understands'.

The second theme, peacemaking, enshrined in the seventh Beatitude, is even more widespread in medieval literature than that the wise shall consort with the wise and leave fools alone. In Old English, several texts associated with Wulfstan, and combining homiletic with legal morality, furnish examples. "Episcopus," from *The Institutes of Polity*,[15] has: "He [*scil.* se bisceop] sceall georne saca sehtan 7 fri∂ wyrcan mid þam woruld deman þe riht lufian."[16] Superficially the manner of *Polity* in its injunctions and admonitions to bishops is not unlike the Exeter *Maxims* in the passages under discussion; there is no such similarity in Wulfstan's homiletic usage. In his phrasing *som* (whence *seman*) is separated from *sacu*, but alliteration seems to connect the two phrases like half-lines in verse forming a long line:

> and beo on þam halgan tidan
> eallswa hit riht is
> eallum cristenum mannum

15. Liebermann 1 (n. 12 above) 477 [*Episc.* 4]. See Karl Jost, *Die "Institutes of Polity, Civil and Ecclesiastical"*, Swiss Studies in English 47 (Bern 1959) 23–24 on the relationship of this text to Wulfstan.

16. 'He [the bishop] shall eagerly settle strife and bring about peace with [such] temporal judges as may love justice'. Liebermann does not comment on the form of *lufian*, presumably with *-ian* for *-ien* subjunctive (on the use of the subjunctive in relative clauses, see Hans Glunz, *Die Verwendung des Konjunktivs im Altenglischen*, Beiträge zur englischen Philologie 11 (Leipzig 1930) 37–68, especially 49, for exemplification amounting to a condition [translated by me 'such . . . as may . . .']; cf. Tauno F. Mustanoja, *A Middle English Syntax* 1, Mémoires de la Société Néophilologique de Helsinki 23 (Helsinki 1960) 461. Alternatively, *-ian* is an error for *-ia∂* in an indicative relative construction; the assumption of error seems unnecessary, but may underlie Liebermann's translation; cf. also Benjamin Thorpe, *Ancient Laws and Institutes of England* (London 1840) 426 (folio edition) or 2.313 (quarto edition). See note 23 below for a similar construction. In their interesting discussion of *sceal* in Old English maxims, Stanley B. Greenfield and Richard Evert attempt to isolate which of the hortatory, monitory, or peremptory senses might apply ("*Maxims II*: Gnome and Poem," in *Anglo-Saxon Poetry: Essays in Appreciation for John C. McGalliard*, ed. Lewis E. Nicholson and Dolores W. Frese [Notre Dame 1975] 337–54). Wulfstan's uses of the verb seem to indicate that we should not attempt to isolate one strand of meaning where all are satisfactory: the use of the subjunctive in relative clauses after *sceal* in the main clause gives no conclusive answer to their problem.

sib and sóm gemæne
and ælc sacu getwæmed.[17]

Wulfstan writes very similarly in the following quotation, but
with the interposition of the phrase *æfter godes rice* between
and deliberately separating two pairs of phrases alliterating on
s, so that it is not wise to connect, as in the earlier quotation
above (*sib and sóm gemæne / and ælc sacu getwæmed*):

and habban us gemæne
sibbe and some
æfter godes rihte
and ælce sace sehtan
swa we eornost magon.[18]

When we turn away from Old English verse and go to the
prose we can find parallels for the wisdom of peacemaking
legally conceived, but there are no verbal parallels in Old
English prose for *þing gehegan*, that is for the instituting of a
meeting, whether technically juridical or not, at which to settle
strife. The nearest that phrase approaches to lawyer's terms is
in the Exeter *Maxims*; and, as we have seen, the use in
Beowulf is far from the uses of the phrase elsewhere: it is less
literal. One reads Edward B. Irving's comments on the passage with some surprise, therefore, especially since his book
gives us on the whole a persuasive reading of the poem. As we
make our incursions into Old English poetry with Modern
English as our base, our lines of communication are stretched
far, too far for success in literary criticism such as is here
exemplified by Irving: "That the fight with Grendel is described in lawyer's terms, after all this violence, is typical of
Anglo-Saxon irony."[19] The evidence of the extant texts does

17. 'and peace and concord be in common to all Christian people as it is
right in that holy season, and every strife at an end'. A. S. Napier, ed.,
Wulfstan . . . Homilien (Berlin 1883) 118; reprinted in Berlin, Zurich, and
Dublin, 1966, with an appendix by Klaus Ostheeren, q.v., 334-36. I have
marked off the phrases; cf. Angus McIntosh, "Wulfstan's Prose," *Proceedings of the British Academy* 35 (1949) 109-42.

18. 'and let us have peace and concord in common according to God's
Law, and settle every strife as we can most earnestly'. Napier (n. 17 above)
272; Ostheeren, 357-58—this part undoubtedly by Wulfstan.

NB

19. Edward B. Irving, *A Reading of Beowulf* (New Haven 1968) 63; cf.
my review, *Notes and Queries* 214 (1969) 35-37.

not support what he says of "lawyer's terms" in Old English; and irony, Anglo-Saxon or other, is not as easily demonstrated as asserted when the facts provide no firm grounds in a context where, as we have seen, the ice of our solid knowledge is too thin for the execution of explicative figures in daring skating.

The same is true of a unique use, *seonoþ gehegan*, at *Phoenix* 493, though its context is much easier:

> wile fæder engla,
> sigora soðcyning,   seonoþ gehegan,
> duguða dryhten,   deman mid ryhte.[20]
> (*Phoenix* 492-94)

The Last Judgment is nowhere else in Old English called *seonoþ*;[21] and, unlike *þing* and *mæðel*, the word is borrowed from Latin (*synodus*), and therefore its collocations cannot go back to the common Germanic poetic language which certainly goes back to pre-Christian times. As we have seen, the Old English word *gehegan* does not occur in legal texts at all, and *mæðel* and *þing* in the sense 'assembly' are very rare indeed in Anglo-Saxon legal texts, though *þing* is a common word in the laws and elsewhere in other senses, namely those, not always to be precisely determined in their contexts, of Latin *causa*, with which may be compared the semantic developments of French *chose* (the etymon of which is *causa*) as well as (derivative and cognate of Old English *þing*) English *thing* and German *Ding* and (derivative and cognate of Old English *sacu*) English *sake* and German *Sache*.

The only Anglo-Saxon legal text where *þing* 'assembly' and also *mæðel* with the same sense occur is the very early Kentish

20. 'The Father of angels, true King of victories, Lord of hosts, will hold a synod, judge righteously'.

21. Cf. N. F. Blake, ed., *The Phoenix* (Manchester 1964) 82, note on line 493, and the references there given. Cf. Hugh S. MacGillivray, *The Influence of Christianity on the Vocabulary of Old English*, Studien zur englischen Philologie 8 (Halle 1902) 32 § 33. F. Liebermann, *The National Assembly in the Anglo-Saxon Period* (Halle 1913) 12 (2.16), holds that Old English *seonoð* is "A very frequent name for the national assembly," i.e., it can be a secular assembly as well as an ecclesiastical council.

Laws of Hlothære and Eadric:[22] "Gif man oþerne sace tihte 7
he þane mannan mote an medle oþþe an þinge, symble se man
þam oðrum byrigean geselle 7 þam riht awyrce þe to hiom
Cantwara deman gescrifen."[23] The phrase *an medle oþþe an
þinge* means 'in assembly' perhaps of two kinds, but probably,
as in my translation, rather of one kind to be described by
either or both of two synonyms. The antiquity of the terms and
their collocation is hardly in doubt. Ancient usage seems to be
involved also in the compound *mæðelfrið* found once only, and
that in an ostensibly even earlier Kentish legal text, the
opening of The Laws of Æthelberht, the first item in the
Textus Roffensis. The reading has suffered damage, but had
been transcribed in the late sixteenth century as *Mœthl friþ*.[24]
Though the reading is in some doubt,[25] its meaning as a form
of peace is clear: we are dealing with the peace of public assembly, violation of which is to be punished.

The people on the continent whose speech is nearest to that
of the English are the Frisians, and of the peoples in England
none is nearer to the Frisians than the inhabitants of Kent,[26]

22. See note 12 above.

23. 'If one man charges another with an offense and he meets that man in
council or assembly, let the [accused] man in every case provide a surety for
the other [*scil.* the plaintiff] and effect [such] justice for him as the judges of
Kentishmen prescribe'. Liebermann (n. 12 above) 1.10 [Hl 8], and note
3.20–21. For the use of the subjunctive, *gescrifen*, see note 16 above.

24. The leaves preceding that on the recto of which the damaged reading
occurs are post-medieval. For the text, see Liebermann (n. 12 above) 1.3
[*Abt* 1 and footnote 5]; for the sense, see 3.4–5, s. *Abt* 1, footnote 12.

25. Cf. Peter Sawyer, ed., *Textus Roffensis* 1, Early English Manuscripts
in Facsimile 7 (Copenhagen 1957) 20/2. It is very unlikely that the
transcriber Francis Tate could, in 1589, have had the knowledge to make up
the reading; cf. Thorpe (n. 16 above) 1 (folio) and 1.2–3 (quarto).

26. See Sir F. H. Stenton, *Anglo-Saxon England* (3rd ed. Oxford 1971)
chapters 1 and 2; M. L. Samuels, "Kent and the Low Countries: Some Lin-
guistic Evidence," in *Edinburgh Studies in English and Scots*, ed. A. J.
Aitken, Angus McIntosh and Hermann Pálsson (London 1971) 3–19; cf.
R. G. Collingwood and J. N. L. Myres, *Roman Britain and the English
Settlements* (Oxford 1937) chapter 20; and see D. M. Wilson's summary of
the historical evidence for the period of the Anglo-Saxon settlement, s.
"Angelsachsen," in Heinrich Beck et al.'s new edition of Johannes Hoops's
Reallexikon der Germanischen Altertumskunde 1 (Berlin 1973), especially

though of mixed descent with an important, archeologically clearly discernible, Frankish constituent element.[27] As Liebermann pointed out when he accepted the post-medieval evidence for *Mœthl friþ* in the early Kentish laws, the Frisians have a word corresponding to it in their extensive laws, *thingfretho*,[28] both in the *Seventeen Küren*, probably of the twelfth century though preserved in manuscripts of which none is earlier than about 1300.[29] Old Frisian legal texts preserve equivalents of *þing gehegan*, namely *heia thing* (and variants).[30] Ancient attribution of much in the Frisian laws to King Charles (that is Charlemagne) tells us more about thirteenth-

---

307. Professor Fred C. Robinson has drawn my attention to the very relevant paper by H. H. Munske, "Angelsächsischaltfriesische Beziehungen in der Rechtsterminologie für Missetaten," in the Wybren J. Buma festschrift, *Flecht op 'e Koai*, Fryske Akademy 382 (Groningen 1970) 40–52.

27. See V. I. Evison, *The Fifth-Century Invasions South of the Thames* (London 1965) passim, but especially chapters 1 and 6.

28. For Frisian I use throughout Karl von Richthofen, *Friesische Rechtsquellen* (Berlin 1840), to which access is convenient through his *Altfriesisches Wörterbuch* (Göttingen 1840). Where available I quote from more recent editions of individual texts because Richthofen is sparing in his annotations of these frequently difficult, technical texts. For the present very limited and purely lexical study, Richthofen's texts seem accurate enough, though their accuracy has been impugned: see Jelle Hoekstra, *Die gemeinfriesischen Siebzehn Küren*. Diss. Groningen (Assen 1940) 40; and F. Buitenrust Hettema's criticism listed by Hoekstra, 195 n. 78.

29. Karl von Richthofen, *Untersuchungen über Friesische Rechtsgeschichte* 1 (Berlin 1880) 66; and still accepted by Jelle Hoekstra, *De eerste en de tweede Hunsinger Codex*, Oudfriese Taal- en Rechtsbronnen 6 (The Hague 1950) 43; *thingfretho* occurs at 50, II.77–78. For other manuscripts and early prints of the same text, see the same editor's Groningen dissertation (n. 28 above) 108–10, lines 141–42; the word occurs also in the Brokmer Laws preserved in two manuscripts, the earlier of which (Oldenburg) is probably also of about 1300, or even earlier according to their editor Wybren J. Buma, *Die Brokmer Rechtshandschriften*, Diss. Groningen (The Hague 1949) 7*; the later (Hanover) is dated 1345 (see Buma 12*). The word occurs at 77–78 line 3, and is discussed at pp. 278–79, with a reference to the discussion of what 'dingfriede' means, by Rudolf His, *Das Strafrecht der Friesen im Mittelalter* (Leipzig 1901) 136–37. Richthofen gives a later occurrence in the Westergo Laws, "Küren vom Wymbritzeradeel" of about 1404 (preserved in a fifteenth-century manuscript), *Rechtsquellen* (n. 28 above) 502/2, line 38 *tingferde*.

30. See Richthofen, *Altfriesisches Wörterbuch* (n. 28 above) s.v. *heia*.

century and perhaps earlier patriotic piety among the Frisians than about linguistic details such as when formulation might have taken place. Yet the impression that, at least in some of the edicts especially in the *Seventeen Küren*, some of the legal formulas are ancient is probably not false. Gradual replacement of *heia* in an alliterative formula by different alliterative formulas makes it likely that what is being replaced had ceased to be familiar. A striking example of such replacement is to be traced by comparing the wording of the First Hunsingo Codex with other versions. The First Hunsingo Codex has:

> Thet is thet formeste lond-riucht alra Fresena, thet alra monna hwelic a sine gode bisitte vnberawad, hit ne se thet ma hine mith tele and mith rethe and mith riuchte thingathe urwinne; ief-tha hit ni se thet hi[31] tha thria liud-thing ursitte ther him thi frana fon thes kenenges halwm beden se to heiane[31] and te haldane, and nelle novder retzia ni riuchta ni deithinges bidia ni wardia.[32]

The alliterative phrase *to heiane and te haldane (thing)* has all the appearance of being ancient, though there is no way of

31. MS *hia . . . heinnane*; cf. the variant reading *te heiane an te haldane*, in *De eerste Emsinger Codex*, ed. Pieter Sipma, Oudfriesche Taal- en Rechtsbronnen 4 (The Hague 1943) 62, IV.5.

32. 'This is the first decree of all the Frisians, that each and every man possess his property without dispute, unless he is convicted by accusation and charge and by regular process; or unless he misses three folk-things which the frana on behalf of the king is commanded to summon and hold for him, and will neither pay what is due nor clear himself nor seek a day of appearance nor attend'.

The text, quoted with some alteration in word-division and punctuation, is that of Hoekstra's edition (n. 29 above) 134, XI.1-8; cf. Richthofen, *Rechtsquellen* (n. 28 above) 40, lines 1-15; the translation and the emendations (see note 31) are indebted to Wybren J. Buma and Wilhelm Ebel, *Das Hunsingoer Recht*, Altfriesische Rechtsquellen 4 (Göttingen 1969) 30–31. For a convenient discussion of the term *frana* (in effect, the president of the court), cf. Siebs (n. 8 above) 67–68; the *frana* is attended by the *asega*, a court official whose function is like that of the dempster in earlier Scots law (Sydney Fairbanks, *The Old West Frisian Skeltana Riucht* [Cambridge Mass. 1939] 22–25, discusses the term *asega* and translates it 'lawsayer', a coinage which well describes the function; for an excellent recent discussion, see Heinrich Beck and Gerhard Köbler, s.v. in the new "Hoops" [n. 26 above] 1.454–57).

proving that, since it has no parallel in any other Germanic language. Indeed the antiquity of the Frisian laws is often thought to be demonstrable by reference to the frequent alliterative phrases in them, as if later ages could not have produced anything like it in occasional alliteration and even rhyme—though in English there are at the very end of the Middle Ages rhyming charters with occasional alliteration designed, presumably, to convey an echo of Anglo-Saxon practice which they purport to represent, of which the following phrases are a few examples: *ever and ay, fight in feeld, That the man in mansing es* (text doubtful), *mansed man, The mercy of the misdeéd, sok and sake, tol and theam* (a very different but related version *tol and tem*), *wit ye wéol*; and from another poem, *hart & hynde, hounds for to hould, stub and stocke.*[33] Survival of alliterative phrasing is no evidence of early composition in English, and need not be in Old Frisian. Replacement in actively used legal texts of an alliterative phrase by another is, however, a sign of obsolescence of the replaced phrase. The First Hunsingo Codex of perhaps the fourteenth century and the First Emsingo Codex of about 1400 have (with slight variation) *to heiane an te haldane*;[34] the phrase is replaced in the Rüstringen MS of about 1300 by *to hebbande and to haldande*, and in the mid-sixteenth-century Westerlau transcript in which the text of a lost manuscript of about 1464 has come down to us, it is replaced by *to halden*

---

33. Moritz Heyne, "Allitterierende Verse und Reime in den friesischen Rechtsquellen," *Germania* 9 (1864) 437–49, differentiates between the most ancient Frisian texts with the best-constructed alliterative verses and the later texts with worse verses. A much more cautious reference to the antiquity of alliterative formulas still remains in Amira-Eckhardt (n. 6 above) 1.221; but see the cautious discussion by Rudolf His, "Die Ueberlieferung der friesischen Küren und Landrechte," *Zeitschrift der Savigny-Stiftung für Rechtsgeschichte*, Germanistische Abt. 20 [= *Zeitschrift für Rechtsgeschichte* 33] (1899) 42–43. The English phrases, which in the way they are used constitute what Heyne, had he known them, would have regarded as worse and more recent practice, are drawn from the late Middle English "rhyming charters," edited by Earle (n. 8 above) 435–40.

34. See note 31 above; cf. Wybren J. Buma and Wilhelm Ebel, *Das Emsiger Recht*, Altfriesische Rechtsquellen 3 (Göttingen 1967) 28.

ende to heren.[35] The phrase *thing heia and halda* is, however, still found in the *Fivelgo Busstaxen* preserved in a manuscript written after 1427.[36] It is not unusual for an obsolescent phrase to be still found in writings after the time, sometimes long after the time, when its obsolescence is attested by replacement elsewhere. It looks as if in Frisian the word *heia* was restricted in currency in the course of the later Middle Ages; in English the cognate *gehegan* had ceased to be used as a legal term, but survived in poetry. As a legal term *heia thing* was very common in the Frisian laws: it may have existed in English too. We have no modern equivalent for the situation as it existed, if that is right, in Old English verse.

Further evidence that Old English *þing gehegan* goes back to the inherited diction of the Germanic tribes and was not in origin poetic only is provided by Old Icelandic, where *heyja þing* is well attested, as are similar legal phrases using *heyja* in combination with words including *dóm*, *leið*, and *sókn*,[37] all in use in technically legal texts. Old Frisian *heia* is not recorded in collocation with *dom*; the cognate of Old Icelandic *sókn*, that is, *sekne* (plural), is too different in sense to admit of the collocation with *heia* in Old Frisian; and there is nothing in Frisian to correspond to the Icelandic legal term *leið*. For one reason or another, therefore, only *þing gehegan* is common to the three languages.

In Old Frisian, however, the collocation of *heia* with *synuth* is common, not—as in the Old English *Phoenix*—in metaphorical use the overtones of which are difficult for us to hear, but used quite literally. That the phrase is common is the

35. 'to have and to hold' and 'to hold and to hear'. The texts are conveniently set out by Richthofen, *Rechtsquellen* (n. 28 above) 40-41; cf. Wybren J. Buma and Wilhelm Ebel, *Das Rüstringer Recht*, Altfriesische Rechtsquellen 1 (Göttingen 1963) 42.

36. See Richthofen, *Rechtsquellen* (n. 28 above) 307/2, lines 26-27; cf. His, "Ueberlieferung" (n. 33 above) 41, for the date of the manuscript. On the term *Busstaxen*, see Klaas Nauta, *Die altfriesischen allgemeinen Busztaxen*, Diss. Groningen (Assen 1941) 11.

37. See Richard Cleasby and Gudbrand Vigfusson, *An Icelandic-English Dictionary* (2nd ed. with supplement by Sir William A. Craigie, Oxford 1957) s.v. *heyja*.

result of the fact that the legal constitution of the Frisians included a well-developed and administratively important system of synodal law with synodal courts under the jurisdiction of the bishops of the area, those of Utrecht and Münster and the Archbishop of Bremen.[38] The bishops' jurisdiction in the ecclesiastical courts corresponds to that of the courts in the secular courts. The correspondence of ecclesiastical *synuth* to secular *thing* underlies such expressions as, in the First Rüstring Text of the *Seventeen Küren*,[39] *anda ena heida synuthe / Tha ena heida thinge* ('at a convened [i.e., public] synod or a convened thing'), where the variant versions have significant differences: the Second Hunsingo Text confines its wording to the *thing*, and the Codex Unia, the wording of which is preserved for us only because Junius transcribed it,[40] has instead *jefta an hetena thinge jefta an ene bannena senethe* ('either at a summoned thing or at a commanded[41] synod'). Mention of both thing and synod together is, however, less common than statements referring to the proper constituting of the synod without mention of the thing, in such phrases as *thet synuth is eheid*, 'the synod is summoned', for example in the Rüstring Synodal Laws.[42] The relationship of the secular to the ecclesiastical courts was a prominent feature of Frisian legal constitution. A system of synodal law obtained among the Franks,[43] but there are, of course, no texts in the vernacu-

38. See the convenient discussion by Siebs (n. 8 above) 96–100.

39. See Hoekstra's Groningen dissertation (n. 28 above) 120, lines 221–22; cf. Richthofen, *Rechtsquellen* (n. 28 above) 29/1, lines 9–10; both editions print parallel texts. See also Buma and Ebel, *Das Rüstringer Recht* (n. 35 above) 42.

40. See Falconer Madan et al., *A Summary Catalogue of Western Manuscripts in the Bodleian Library at Oxford* 2.2 (Oxford 1937) 975–76 for MS Junius 49, and 985 for MS Junius 109. From Theodor Siebs (*Westfriesische Studien*, Abhandlungen der Königlichen Akademie der Wissenschaften zu Berlin, Philosophisch-historische Abhandlung nicht zur Akademie gehörender Gelehrter 2 [Berlin 1895]) it appears that the Codex Unia, of the late fifteenth century, is not likely to have been a uniform work.

41. See Siebs, *Grundlagen und Aufbau* (n. 8 above) 89, for how a synod or a thing may have been proclaimed.

42. See Richthofen, *Rechtsquellen* (n. 28 above) 128/2, line 14; Buma and Ebel, *Das Rüstringer Recht* (n. 35 above) 114 § 8.

43. See O. M. Dalton, *The History of the Franks by Gregory of Tours* 1

lar in which we might find expressions cognate with *þing gehegan* or *seonoþ gehegan*. In England synodal jurisdiction was limited and operated in cases involving ecclesiastics, but never extended as in Friesland to secular jurisdiction; there was not even, it seems, a single, unambiguous term for the ecclesiastical courts, and Latin *synodus* and the Old English forms like *sinoþ* in Wulfstan's *Institutes of Polity* do not arise by substitution of synod for thing in the inherited legal diction.[44] As we have seen, the poetic phrase *þing gehegan* may well be part of the inherited vocabulary of the Anglo-Saxons, poetic in Old English, a language in which *þing* 'assembly' was obsolescent in prose; and in Frisian, a language in which no early poetry is preserved, cognate *heia thing* is legal only.

While there is no doubt about the meaning of the phrase *seonoþ gehegan* of *Phoenix* 493, we have nothing to go on to tell us how it came into being in the language. There is, of course, good evidence that throughout the Anglo-Saxon period there was close contact between the Frisians and the Anglo-Saxons. The historical evidence of Frisians in King Alfred's navy is supplemented by numismatic evidence, and further by the literary evidence of the Exeter *Maxims* (93–106) on how the Frisian's loving wife cherishes her husband—a happy marriage of members of the two nations, celebrated in poetry.[45] It is possible, in view of these close contacts, that the correspondence of Old English poetic *seonoþ gehegan* to Old Frisian legal *heia synuth* is a borrowing into Old English of an

(2 vols. Oxford 1927) 302–13. The nature of the Frankish synods is, however, different from that of the Frisian synodal courts. The Frisian ecclesiastical courts, i.e. their synodal courts to which they apply the word *synuth*, are analogous to their secular courts, i.e. their counts' courts, whereas the Frankish synods are Church councils operating in a different system; see Hans Barion, *Das fränkisch-deutsche Synodalrecht des Frühmittelalters*, in A. M. Koeniger's Kanonistische Studien und Texte 5–6 (Bonn 1931).

44. See Liebermann, *Die Gesetze* (n. 12 above) 2.437–41, s.v. *Geistliches Gericht*. See Wulfstan's *Polity*, ed. Jost (n. 15 above) 178–216, especially *De synodo*, 210–16.

45. For the historical evidence, especially the numismatic evidence, see Stenton (n. 26 above) 57 and 221; cf. *Anglo-Saxon Chronicle*, A.D. 897, for Frisians in King Alfred's navy; see *Two of the Saxon Chronicles Parallel*, ed. John Earle and Charles Plummer 2 (2 vols. Oxford 1892–99) 111–12. For the

Old Frisian phrase. The original audience could have known what we can never know, if the poet has borrowed from continental synodal law his term for the Last *Sendgericht* ('synodal court'). If so, he has by a daring neologism, calqued on the closely related language of Germanic continental canon law, found words for the divine Last Synod where bishops themselves shall have cause to tremble before the throne of the highest priestly Judge. But we cannot be sure. In a much less metaphorical view, the Last Judgment, with its various classes of participants ranged in order, is not unlike a great Church council under the presidency of the Almighty, specifically referred to in *Phoenix* in the half-line following our phrase as *duguða dryhten*, 'Lord of Hosts'. Much of the context of the use of *gehegan ðing* in *Beowulf* is obscure and there is little in it to help us understand that passage with assurance that we are doing with it as the original audience did. Here in *Phoenix*, the context is as clear as anything in Old English, and we still lack that assurance as we try to understand *seonoþ gehegan*. Where the higher flights of literary criticism lack the breath of contextual knowledge to support it, a more terrestrially bound, philological view seems safer, though perhaps unjust to the poet's skill: he, looking for an ecclesiastical equivalent of secular *þing gehegan*, poetic only in his language, rummaged about and thought *seonoþ gehegan* suitable, and suitably vague for a grand council in a language the laws of which had no established phraseology for that sort of thing.

Exact understanding of words in their context is a prerequisite of literary criticism; and often we lack that understanding for Old English.

---

interpretation of the Exeter *Maxims* 93–106, see George P. Krapp and Elliott V. K. Dobbie, eds., *The Anglo-Saxon Poetic Records* 3 (New York 1936) 160 (text), and 306 (notes); as Krapp and Dobbie say, "the prominence of the Frisians as a seafaring folk in the early Middle Ages makes a geographical allusion here [line 95 *Frysan wif*] not improbable." Since the Frisians were the seafarers and the marital home with the loving wife is, in contrast with the roving husband, a fixed abode, the interpretation that *Frysan* is genitive, 'of the Frisian', seems preferable to taking it as a dative adjective weak, '(to the) Frisian', qualifying *wife* dative, as does Williams (n. 13 above) 138.

ESTHETICS AND MEANING AND THE
TRANSLATION OF OLD ENGLISH POETRY

Stanley B. Greenfield

IN THE PRECEDING ESSAY, E. G. Stanley convincingly
demonstrates the occasional (or even-more-than-occasional)
inexactitude in our comprehension of the meanings of Old English words, an inexactitude that renders literary criticism pre-
carious, if not parlous. He persuasively argues further that some
sound effects can only be assessed impressionistically by modern critics, since the dialects in which the poems have been
transmitted are not necessarily those in which they were
composed. Cautionary also is he about the deceptive significance of etymologies in establishing word-meanings, about the
frequent difficulties of Old English syntax, about the imposi-
tion of larger esthetic designs (like irony) in dubious context.
One might observe that such caveats are not exclusive to the
problems of Old English poetry: we need only think of the
notorious *buckle* of Hopkins's *Windhover* or the portly (?) jar
("of a port in air") of Wallace Stevens's *Anecdote*. But a critic
must do the best he can with such uncertainties and must state
his opinions with some assurance, even if he does "skate on
thin ice." Of course he should be honest with his readers,
giving pros and cons, weighing the expectations and implications that lead to his evaluative decisions.[1] How appropriate it
would be were there an Old English maxim giving the *sceal* of
the literary critic.

1. See my *The Interpretation of Old English Poems* (London and Boston
1972) especially 30–59.

91

My concern is with a special aspect of literary criticism that must come to terms with the difficulties of meaning: the critical act that inheres in the translation of poetry into poetry, that is, of Old English poetry into modern English poetic form. Many have been the attempts to give us satisfying translations of Old English poems, and several the explanations of the translation process, with comments on the shortcomings of previous attempts and the constraints upon meter and diction to capture the flavor of the original. Problems of meter and diction have, in fact, been the main considerations of most poetic translators, to the slighting of other esthetic components. It is the total relationship of esthetics to meaning, and the possibility of reconstituting that relationship in modern poetic translations of Old English poetry, that I should like to consider more closely. I will go so far as to suggest that the esthetics of a poem *cannot* be separated from its meaning and that closer attention to esthetics can often help clarify even the literal meaning of words in their contexts. I shall attempt to demonstrate by my own poetic translations and by analyses of their responsiveness to the esthetics-*cum*-meaning of their Old English originals that even the meaning of *Beowulf* 419-26, a quicksand for interpretation, as Stanley has shown, *can* be more firmly fixed than he allows––at least to the extent that a reasonable poetic translation of it can be made. Such poetic translations as I propose demand, of course, not only a critical sensitivity to Old English word meanings and poetic style but a certain poetic talent and understanding of modern English poetry.[2] To feel that one has the requisite sensitivity, talent, and understanding must surely be the last infirmity of the scholarly mind; from what follows it will be all too clear that I have succumbed to that malaise. I can only hope my readers will find some signs of health, if not in me, at any rate for the

2. Cf. Jean Paris's comment: "[The act of poetic translation] requires primarily a deep insight into the nature of the work, which means the translator has to be a critic, an analyst as well as a linguist and a poet, too"—in his "Translation and Creation," *The Craft and Context of Translation: A Symposium*, ed. William Arrowsmith and Roger Shattuck (Austin Tex. 1961) 57-67 at 62.

transmission of the vitality of Old English poetry to our own age.

This is hardly the occasion to trace the development of translations of Old English poetry, let alone the general problems of poetic translation.[3] But in general, the translator either tries to recapture what is to his contemporaries "archaic" and thus make the poem a museum piece refurbished for those ignorant of the original language and meaning, or he tries to recreate anew, in the spirit of his own idiom and age, a poem *after* the original. In the preface to his mid-twentieth century translation of *Beowulf*, Edwin Morgan nicely summarizes and scores earlier efforts of both types: in the 19th and early 20th centuries he comments on "the neomedievalism of Morris and the Pre-Raphaelites, late Victorian romanticism, the aestheticism of the nineties, the mild-mannered prettiness and sentiment of the pre-Georgian and Georgian poets"; post-World War I translators he criticizes for failure "to establish a contact with the poetry of their time."[4] Speaking specifically of the diction employed by poetic translators of *Beowulf*, Morgan decries the traces of archaic diction that still becloud the efforts of even a Charles W. Kennedy or a Mary Waterhouse, for, he says, such diction is supererogatory given "the inescapable bedrock vocabulary of *king, lord,* and *retinue, gold-giving* and *mead-drinking, coat of mail* and *dragon* and *burial-mound* [which] the twentieth-century reader will find enough . . . remote from his own experience without any superadded linguistic crinkum-crankum and mock-epopeanism."[5] Considering also the metrical problem in translating Old English verse, he dismisses as inadequate such previous measures as

3. For a bibliography of studies of the translation process with respect to Old English poetry, see items 1389–1409 in the forthcoming *A Bibliography of Publications on Old English Literature* by Stanley B. Greenfield and Fred C. Robinson (Toronto). For the problems connected with translation in general, see among others the Arrowsmith and Shattuck volume mentioned in n. 2, above, and the collection of essays in *On Translation*, ed. Reuben A. Brower (Cambridge Mass. 1959).

4. Edwin Morgan, *Beowulf: A Verse Translation into Modern English* (Aldington Kent 1952) vii–viii.

5. Ibid. xi–xii.

blank verse, rhyming syllabic meters, and "imitative" stress-meters with or without the strict Anglo-Saxon alliterative scheme. What is wanted, he declares, for the modern equivalent of the *Beowulf* metrics is a "gravity and 'hardness' . . . [something] wary, reconnoitring, anfractuous, and often quantal or multidimensional. . . . Harshness must be risked. . . . The lines must be able to contract to terseness, and expand to splendour."[6] A free four-stress line is Morgan's solution, with no strict alliterative pattern.

Morgan's translation is a good one, and if I have reservations about it they may be attributed to the passage of almost forty years, the encroachment of new epochal and personal sensibilities, and the wealth of critical insight about the poem that has accumulated in that time. Before turning to my own "intentions" as a poetic translator, however, I should like to look at a more recent non-literalist of the translative imagination for the insights he has added, by practice and precept, to our understanding of the relationship between esthetics and meaning in the process of poetic recreation. Burton Raffel, even more than Morgan, has attempted in his translations to write *poems* that a modern audience will find comprehensible, delightful, and tuned to its own esthetic sensibilities. He does not wish, like many earlier and some modern-day translators, "to take one through the looking glass back into the original poem," but rather to bring the original into the world of modern readers, relying upon current idioms, syntax, lexicon, and poetic traditions.[7] If he must sacrifice fidelity to the original word-meanings or esthetic techniques for a contemporary stylistic recreation, he will, with Wilde's Algy, be content with "style." Thus he will have no truck with outmoded and conventional Old English poetic features such as orality or formulaic repetition or kennings, because they "are not expressions

6. Ibid. xvi. Cf. William Arrowsmith, "The Lively Conventions of Translation," *Craft and Context* (n. 2 above) 122–40 at 128, 137ff.

7. Burton Raffel, *The Forked Tongue: A Study of the Translation Process* (The Hague 1971) 11. Raffel's theory seems to be opposed to that of Ezra Pound's "interpretive translation" concept; for an excellent critique of Pound's translation of the Old English *Seafarer*, see John Hollander, "Ver-

which fit into the tone and texture of the modern English equivalent" he wishes to create.[8]

One may quarrel with Raffel's recreative freedom—and I will; for poetic translations, it seems to me, must somehow, however free, capture the essential spirit and esthetic quality, *mutatis mutandis*, of the original in a way that Raffel's often do not.[9] Nevertheless, Raffel *has* in some measure brought a proper creativity to the art of such translation as Robert Creed, in his foreword to Raffel's *Poems from the Old English*, demonstrates:

> At times the reader of Old English who turns to compare Mr. Raffel's text with the "originals" will find, for example, that "the *hands* that carved 'The Husband's Message'" (line 14) are not to be found. Line 13 reads, in the Krapp/Dobbie text, simply *se þisne beam agrof*: "he [who] this wood carved." The Old English scholar may be ready to chide Mr. Raffel for his "addition" when he suddenly sees the *rightness* of these "hands" and turns his chiding into praise for the poet who has *opened out, displayed more fully*, the hint enclosed in the image *agrof*.
>
> [Or] line 42 of "The Seafarer" reads *þæt he a his sæfore sorge næbbe*: "that he ever [in] his sea-faring sorrow does not have." Mr. Raffel makes of this the following: "That he feels no fear as the sails unfurl." Now "the sails" do not "unfurl" in the Old English line—indeed, they are not even there. Yet in a deeper sense they *are* there, quietly waiting for the poet's ear to hear them, in *sæfore*, and Mr. Raffel's ear has heard the hint.

---

sions, Interpretations, and Performances," *On Translation* (n. 3 above) 210–12.

8. Raffel (n. 7 above) 26.

9. Cf. Jackson Matthews, who would agree with Raffel's cry for "freedom" in translation, but who imposes an important limitation thereon: "To translate a poem whole is to compose another poem. A whole translation will be faithful to the *matter*, and it will 'approximate the form,' of the original; and it will have a life of its own, which is the voice of the translator. . . . In the 'approximation of form' . . . the motive is invention, not imitation. The translator has to invent formal effects in his own language that give a sense of those produced by the original in its own"—"Third Thoughts on Translating Poetry," *On Translation* (n. 3 above) 67. Matthew's last sentence is the crucial one.

He has, again, uncoiled for our delight an image too tightly locked into the Old English line, and has set up a subtle, pun-like identification of the unfurling of the sails with the unfurling of fear and wonder.[10]

This seems to me not only legitimate but exciting poetic translation, even if to my taste a little too smooth for the Old English measure. Yet Raffel often fails to pick up *un*hidden esthetic-meaning interplay. For example, in the very verse unit of *The Seafarer* in which he unfurls the sails, he has translated

> But there isn't a man on earth so proud,
> So born to greatness, so bold with his youth,
> Grown so brave, or so graced by God,
> That he feels no fear as the sails unfurl,
> Wondering what Fate has willed and will do.

The original, of course, is as follows:

> for þon nis þæs modwlonc   mon ofer eorþan,
> ne his gifena þæs god,   ne in geoguþe to þæs hwæt,
> ne in his dædum to þæs deor,   ne him his dryhten to þæs hold,
> þæt he a his sæfore   sorge næbbe,
> to hwon hine Dryhten   gedon wille.[11] (39-43)

What Raffel has missed here is the deliberate contrast the Old English poet makes between the earthly *dryhten* whose favor the seafarer (or any-man) may have gained and the heavenly *Dryhten* whose favor he is concerned about on his sea-voyage; and in omitting this interplay Raffel has falsified both the esthetic and meaning of the poem. Perhaps in this connection we might reverse Keats's lines and say that *un*heard melodies are sweet, but *heard* ones are sweeter! Since it is easier to criticize than to create, I might offer in contrast my own rendition of these lines:

> for there's no man on earth so sea-
> soned in spirit, so sure of fortune,
> so graced by youth and a gracious lord,
> that in his sea-faring he has no care
> of what the Lord has in store for him.

10. Robert P. Creed, foreword to Burton Raffel, *Poems from the Old English* (2nd ed. Lincoln Neb. 1964) xi–xii.

11. Ida L. Gordon, ed., *The Seafarer* (London 1960) 38–39.

My *sea-faring* for *sæfore* may unfurl no sails, but perhaps it offers more sustenance for the providential contrast between the fortunes *ofer eorþan* and the literal/symbolic sea which informs the esthetics and meaning of the Old English poem. And the punning I have *sea*-soned my translation with, while not "true to" the original passage in all respects, *is* an esthetic "equivalent," taking the poem as a whole. (I will comment shortly on the metrical scheme of my version.)

For all my misgivings, Raffel's translations are very instructive about esthetics and meaning and the art of poetic translation. What I wish to consider now is his defense of his translation of *Beowulf* 1-11. My comments thereon will lead me into consideration of a number of the stylistic qualities of Old English poetry, a statement of my principles of poetic translation, and some extended samples of my own translations to suggest how such translations may best reflect in modern English verse the interplay of Old English esthetics and meaning.

Though the first eleven lines of *Beowulf* are well enough known, it will not hurt to have them before us:

> Hwæt! We Gardena   in geardagum,
> þeodcyninga,   þrym gefrunon,
> hu ða æþelingas   ellen fremedon.
>   Oft Scyld Scefing   sceaþena þreatum,
> monegum mægþum,   meodosetla ofteah,
> egsode eorlas.   Syððan ærest wearð
> feasceaft funden,   he þæs frofre gebad,
> weox under wolcnum,   weorðmyndum þah
> oðþæt him æghwylc   þara ymbsittendra
> ofer hronrade   hyran scolde,
> gomban gyldan.   Þæt wæs god cyning![12]

Raffel's version of these lines is as follows:

> Hear me! We've heard of Danish heroes,
> Ancient kings and the glory they cut
> For themselves, swinging mighty swords!

12. This and all following quotations of Old English poetry are from George P. Krapp and Elliott V. K. Dobbie, eds., *The Anglo-Saxon Poetic Records* (6 vols. New York *1931*–53). I do not necessarily use their punctuation as the basis of my own translations.

> How Shild made slaves of soldiers from every
> Land, crowds of captives he'd beaten
> Into terror; he'd traveled to Denmark alone,
> An abandoned child, but changed his own fate,
> Lived to be rich and much honored. He ruled
> Lands on all sides: wherever the sea
> Would take them his soldiers sailed, returned
> With tribute and obedience. There was a brave
> King!

This translation was published in 1963 and its "freeness" drew fire from many reviewers. In the reissue of 1971 by the University of Massachusetts Press, Raffel took issue with those reviewers in a section entitled "Postscript—1971."[13] Claiming that they misunderstood "what literary translation itself is all about," he proceeded to demonstrate what his theory of poetic translation is by reference to lines 4–11 of the poem. Citing the Garmonsway et al. literal prose translation,[14] he calls it "a dogged prose rendering," saying that it translates only "information, narrative—and nothing very much more." In that version, he continues, the text is reduced "to a thin wash-drawing of its passing shadow . . . [eliminating the] nuances, associations, images" which make *Beowulf* a great poem. True, to a great extent, but I would suggest that Raffel gives less credit to the Garmonsway translation than it deserves. Following this denigration, Raffel gives his version of the lines I have quoted and argues for the legitimacy of his "free" lexical transformations. For example, he says that *mægðum* (line 5) means "nations, people" as well as "tribes"—though I fail to see that he uses this transformation, since he delivers us "crowds of captives." *Ofteah* (line 5), he avers, means "subjugated, reduced to servitude or slavery" as well as "deprived"—but it only means the former, so far as I can determine, by virtue of this particular context. In fact a little later Raffel says that

13. Burton Raffel, *Beowulf: A New Translation* (New York 1963; repr. Amherst Mass. 1971) xix.

14. George N. Garmonsway, Jacqueline Simpson, and Hilda Ellis Davidson, *Beowulf and its Analogues* (London and New York 1968). Raffel's remarks, summarized and quoted in the next few pages of my text, come from the "Postscript" in his 1971 *Beowulf*, xix–xxi.

"the Old English talks of *meodosetla*, 'mead-hall-seats,' and I talk of 'captives'—but the privilege of a mead-hall-seat was part and parcel of the independent status of a warrior, so that to deprive him of that seat was in fact to deprive him of his freedom": an admission, after all, that *ofteah* does mean "deprived." What Raffel does not admit, or even seem to understand, is that his "captive" translation totally ignores the litotical effect of *meodosetla ofteah*, not to mention its introduction of the significant image, for the poem as a whole, of the hall. *God cyning*, Raffel further contends, means not only an "excellent king" but a "brave, strong, efficient, able king." Agreed; but his translation as "brave king" hardly captures that totality of meaning.

One of the strangest defenses he makes is of his elimination of the kenning *hronrad* (line 10) by transforming it into "sea." He does so, he says, oddly enough, *because* it *is* a kenning, "the Old English formulaic way of using a specific part of something to symbolize the larger entity as well." I find it odd that he censures the "dogged prose" of the Garmonsway translation while himself de-poeticizing a poetic component of the original. (What to do with such kennings in a modern translation *is* something of a problem, to which I shall offer my own solution.) On the other hand, Raffel expands some lexical usages: "The 'sailing' of Shild's soldiers is literally not in the Old English, nor is their 'returning,'" he admits; "but both verbs as physical facts are inherent in the kinds of military successes being described." Apart from the confusion such a statement makes between a part of speech and a "physical fact," its term "soldiers" for the warriors of this poem seems anachronistic; and not only are sailing and returning not literally in the Old English, but neither are the soldiers. The emphasis is on *Scyld*'s deeds, and though of course Scyld performed those deeds with the aid of his warriors, the poet is ignoring *them* to focus on the stature of the king. Raffel has revealed a hidden meaning here that has "sprung" the original esthetic significance.

It is now, however, time to state those principles guiding my own poetic translations. The first is that the translation must not only be attractive to the reader who knows no Old English, but also appeal to anyone familiar with both the poem and the Anglo-Saxon poetic sensibility, insofar as that can be determined. Poetry was and is something of a game, and there is no reason why the translator, who should be something of a gamester, cannot be both accurate (whatever that means in the long run)[15] and so felicitious in his verbal-stylistic choices as to excite and delight both the *lered* and the *lewed*. Second, the translator must not limit himself to a verse-by-verse or even line-by-line translation, but, with King Alfred, proceed sometimes word-by-word, more often sense-by-sense *within the syntactic or rhetorical unit* and with some sense of the poem's *total configuration*. Such a procedure provides the necessary flexibility that many earlier translators of Old English poetry have not allowed themselves. Third, the metrical system must be equivalent to, but not the same as, the Old English alliterative verse:[16] it must be flexible enough to reflect the freedom of our modern poetry yet have a fixity that suggests, but does not ape, the restraint of the four-stress heavily-caesuraed Anglo-Saxon line. It cannot systematically use alliteration in the Old English manner even with such modern examples as Hopkins and Auden before us. To this end I have "invented" a metrical pattern that I think offers the kind of equivalent I have described, which I shall come to in a moment. Fourth, the poetic translator should utilize not only modern stylistic devices and locutions, but also, where appropriate, stylistic, syntactic, and phonological patterns and features found in Old English poems. (This combination of styles will of course entail modifications of formulaic repetition, kennings, and the like, but neither their expunging nor mechanical copying.) Fifth, he should—indeed must—try to unlock the meaning hidden in Old English images, but not at the expense of falsifying the meaning and esthetic contour of the original.

15. Any number of translation studies have dealt with the problem of accuracy: see, e.g., essays by Willard V. Quine and Werner Winter in *On Translation* and *Craft and Context* respectively (nn. 2 and 3 above).

16. Cf. Morgan's comments on metrical equivalency (n. 6 above).

With these principles in mind let us look now at my translation of *Beowulf* 1-11:

> Indeed! We have heard of the glory
> Of Danish kings in former days,
> How princes with spears sped in valor.
> Often Scyld Scefing shattered the hosts,
> Many a mead-hall left unsettled,
> Terrorized tribes, since first as a child
> He was found abandoned; he found
> Recourse for that, growing in worldly
> Honors until all nations near and
> Far over whale-big seas obeyed him,
> Paid tribute: there was a king in-deed!

My metrical system is adapted from Auden's *Hammerfest,* where Auden used alternating lines of thirteen and eleven syllables. My scheme, in case it is not immediately apparent, uses a nine-syllable line for regular Old English verse, and eleven-syllable for hypermetric lines (the latter to be seen in a selection from *Judith*). This number of syllables seems a natural equivalent for the Anglo-Saxon poetic line: it allows for the flexibility of modern verse—the caesura can be placed anywhere from after the first to after the eighth syllable—and yet provides a slight restraint that is suggestive of the fixity of the Old English verse form without simulating that metrical scheme.[17] I have not tried to achieve any regular alliterative pattern; in fact, my first line has no alliteration, but the alliteration builds to a climax through the *Danish* and *days* of line 2 to the intricate phonological patterning of line three. The next line actually copies the Old English alliteration, and then my version moves away from this feature to a more natural or modern sound contour while still preserving, I think, the feel of the Old English alliterative line.

It will be obvious that I have not strictly followed the esthetic contour of this passage. For example, I have used an envelope pattern that is not in the original; nor is the "indeed—in-deed" pun therein involved. Yet envelope patterns and wordplay *are*

17. See further my second comment on a passage from *The Wanderer* later in this essay, and n. 25 below.

part of the Old English esthetic and I think in this case my translations legitimately convey meaning hidden within the Old English images. (It is Scyld's deeds and those of his Danish successors that the poet is *hwaet*-ing with the pluck of his harp.) The etymological pun in my "mead-hall unsettled" may appeal only to the scholar, yet it echoes the litotes of *meodosetla ofteah*. The modern-sounding enjambment of "near and / Far over whale-big seas" and the echoing *tribes* and *tribute* also have their Old English stylistic counterparts. I would call attention to the fact that I have kept an active verb for the *fremedon* of the Old English (line 3), unlike Morgan, who, after chastizing William Ellery Leonard for not placing his verb *fought* in the same position as in the original:

What ho! We've heard the glory   of Spear-Danes, clansmen-kings,
Their deeds of olden story,—   how fought the aethelings,[18]

eschews any verb at all in his version:

> How that glory remains in remembrance,
> Of the Danes and their kings in days gone,
> The acts and valour of princes of their blood!

Further, both Morgan and Raffel continue the *hu* of line 3 into the fourth line of their translations, which is *not* what the Old English does: this continued "how" prolongs the idea of "have heard," upon which it depends, rather than, as the Old English poet has done, moving quickly to bring his audience directly on to the historic scene. On the other hand, it may appear at first blush that I have abandoned the "Spear" of the *Gardena* of line 1 as part of the compound noun, but I have rather delivered it into a syntactic ambiguity in my "How princes with spears sped in valor," giving it a thrust more consonant with modern verse yet not un-Anglo-Saxon in its esthetic quality. Finally, I must confess, I rather like my lexical transformation of the kenning *hronrad* into "whale-big seas," as both modern sounding (unlike the usual translation "whale-road") and expansive in its ambiguity.[19] (I would keep this pattern for the

18. William Ellery Leonard, *Beowulf: A New Verse Translation for Fireside and Class Room* (New York 1923) 3.

19. On the force of *hronrad* here (as opposed to *swanrad* at line 200), see Adrien Bonjour, "On Sea Images in *Beowulf*," *Journal of English and*

translation of kennings as best I can, translating, for example, its counterpart *swanrad*, line 200, as "swan-graced sea.")

Other kinds of passages pose different problems of esthetics and meaning for the translator, and I should like to turn now briefly to some of them. The first is the famous passage in *The Battle of Maldon* where the Vikings cross the Panta (Blackwater):

> Wodon þa wælwulfas   (for wætere ne murnon),
> wicinga werod,   west ofer Pantan,
> ofer scir wæter   scyldas wegon,
> lidmen to lande   linde bæron. (96–99)

Bessinger well describes the phonological intoxication of this passage when he says the poet could not resist continuing the "key of *w*" for the several lines.[20] Raffel's translation in his *Poems from the Old English* seems not at all concerned with the melody of this passage or the part it plays in its meaning:

> So, the sea-wolves, the Norse sailors,
> No longer afraid of the stream, crossed west
> On the Panta, carried their shields over shining
> Water and brought pirates and weapons to land.

My endeavor to capture the sheer movement and sound of the original is quite different:

> Wolves on the move, avid for slaughter,
> Heedless of water the Vikings came,
> Bold sea-men over shining water
> Bore shields west across Panta to shore.

Here I have attempted a combination of *w* and *v* sounds, imitation of the device of variation with "water," and intrusion of various rhyming patterns as a good un-archaized equivalent to the style and meaning of the Old English. Additionally, in the "Bore . . . shore" rhyme of the last verse, bringing the marauders across the *brycg* of the original, I have introduced a kind of chiasmus such as the *Maldon* poet himself used earlier

German Philology 54 (1955), 111–15, repr. in his *Twelve Beowulf Papers, 1940–1960: With Additional Comments* (Neuchatel 1962) 116–17.

20. Jess B. Bessinger, Jr., "*Maldon* and the *Óláfsdrápa*: An Historical Caveat," *Comparative Literature* 14 (1962) 28–29.

when the Viking messenger called across the water to Byrht-
noth:

> Þa *stod on stæðe,*   stiðlice clypode
> wicinga ar,   wordum mælde,
> se on beot abead   brimliþendra
> ærænde to þam eorle,   þær he *on ofre stod.* (25–28)

This kind of conflation of esthetics and meaning, even from
different parts of a poem, will provide, I believe, the excitement and equivalency of the original poem.

The Old English *Judith* offers a still different challenge to
the translator-critic, and I should like to consider next a
hypermetric passage from it—all but the first and last lines—
where I will use eleven rather than nine syllables for a metrical
equivalent. The hypermetric style is not the problem here, but
the high concentration of compound nouns and a sense of
what was a live or a dead image for the Anglo-Saxon audience.
The passage in question is lines 15–22, where Holofernes's
warriors go to the feast he has prepared:

> Hie ða to ðam symle   sittan eodon,
> wlance to wingedrince,   ealle his weagesiðas,
> bealde byrnwiggende.   Þær wæron bollan steape
> boren æfter bencum gelome,   swylce eac bunan ond orcas
> fulle fletsittendum;   hie þæt fæge þegon,
> rofe rondwiggende,   þeah ðæs se rica ne wende,
> egesful eorla dryhten.   Ða wearð Holofernus,
> goldwine gumena,   on gytesalum.

My translation is much freer in some ways than the others I
have presented, but not without some attention to the late
Anglo-Saxon poetic style:

> Putting aside armor, then, proudly,
> Comrades in woe set to the feast, filled up cup
> After cup with wine as they put aside shields,
> Bearing themselves on the benches to a fate
> They could not foresee, so flushed in their spirits:
> Neither the warriors drinking nor their lord,
> The terrorizer of men, Holofernes,
> Gift-giver to men giving good cheer.

The concatenation of compound nouns in this passage—
wingedrince, weagesiðas, byrnwiggende (and its variation
rondwiggende), *fletsittendum, goldwine,* and *gytesalum*—is
part of its stylistic quality; but a literal reproduction of it
would not, in my opinion, pass muster as a modern poetic
effort. Hence my substitution of participial phrases: "putting
aside . . .," "bearing themselves . . .," "so flushed . . .," and
subordinating equivalents. I think they work. More controversial, probably, is my attempt to deliver meaning in the *byrn-
wiggende/rondwiggende* sequence: the "putting aside" of
armor and shields; but my assumption is that these were probably dead metaphors for the poet and his audience, and that
the context of the feast would hardly find the warriors wearing
armor and carrying shields. If these words did suggest something more, my disengagement of the warriors from their
accoutrements is as likely a meaning as any, and it leads
appropriately into the pun on "bearing," a pun that begged to
be born from its esthetic-and-meaning context as did the "so
flushed in their spirits."

Quite different is the style of lines 19–29a of *The Wanderer*
to which I have elsewhere referred as having sweep and majes-
ty.[21] These I have given a more literal translation though not
without, as I hope will be evident, some attempt to fuse esthetics and meaning into my patterned nine-syllable verse. These
I should like to present (I have added in translation lines
29b–36) without either the original Old English or any comments but two:

> So I have often closely confined
> My heart's thoughts, weighted down by woe,
> Bereft of home, bereft of kinsmen,
> Since long ago the lord who gave me gold
> Was given himself to earth's darkness,
> And I dejected departed thence
> Over waves tight bound in wintry mood,
> Over seas' expanse sought in high hall
> A treasured lord, one who might my love

21. Greenfield (n. 1 above) 119; earlier in "Syntactic Analysis and Old
English Poetry," *Neuphilologische Mitteilungen* 64 (1963) 373–78.

Contain, or comfort give me friendless,
Hearten me with joys. He knows who him-
Self has sorrow had as his sole friend
How cruel a lot such a comrade is:
His the dark of exile, not bright gold,
Cold heart, not warmth-enfolding glory:
He recalls the warriors in the hall,
Fair treasure given, how bright feasts were
Before his lord when young—lost now, all!

The first comment concerns my translation of the somewhat ambiguous phrase *waþema gebind*, literally "the binding of waves," whose meaning has generally been taken to indicate the frozen sea. But I am not sure the phrase is not a kenning for the sea itself, that is, the binding of one wave to another to form the surface of the ocean; hence my double translation as "waves tight bound" and "seas' expanse"—a semi-attempt to bring to the surface hidden meaning. The second comment may throw some light on the "rightness" of my nine-syllable line as metrical equivalent. A poet colleague of mine who did not know the Old English, noted that in my translations there was a less-than-normal use of definite and indefinite articles— which the nine-syllable line forces. The binding effect of this syntactic shortening catches the essential metrical quality of the Anglo-Saxon poetic line.

Let us conclude with the *Beowulf* passage which Stanley has so expertly anatomized. He deals in particular with lines 419–26a, but to cope with the problems in their larger esthetic and semantic environment, I should like to back up and include lines 407-18 as well, and it will be convenient to have this whole segment of young Beowulf's opening remarks to Hrothgar before us:

"Wæs þu, Hroðgar, hal!   Ic eom Higelaces
mæg ond magoðegn;   hæbbe ic mærða fela
ongunnen on geogoþe.   Me wearð Grendles þing
410   on minre eþeltyrf   undyrne cuð;
secgað sæliðend   þæt þæs sele stande,
reced selesta,   rinca gehwylcum
idel ond unnyt,   siððan æfenleoht

under heofenes hador   beholen weorþeð.

415   Þa me þæt gelærdon   leode mine
þa selestan,   snotere ceorlas,
þeoden Hroðgar,   þæt ic þe sohte,
forþan hie mægenes cræft   minne cuþon,
selfe ofersawon,   ða ic of searwum cwom,

420   fah from feondum;   þær ic fife geband,
yðde eotena cyn   ond on yðum slog
niceras nihtes,   nearoþearfe dreah,
wraec Wedera nið   (wean ahsodon),
forgrand gramum,   ond nu wið Grendel sceal,

425   wid þam aglæcan,   ana gehegan
ðing wið þyrse."

After following the numerous arguments Stanley presents against the concept of legal implications in the *gehegan ðing* (425b–26a), one is forced to accept his rejection of the irony Irving perceives here. At the same time Stanley does imply that other uses may hint at the sense of an appointed day or time. And I have tried in the act of critical translation to incorporate this suggestion. More than this, I have gone back to Beowulf's opening remarks about the news of *Grendles ðing* reaching him in Geatland. Stanley does not take this into account; yet it forms something of an envelope pattern for this whole section and can be made, in my estimation, through the consideration of that esthetic component, more precisely meaningful than Stanley would allow. I wonder too whether the exact visualization of the various kinds of monsters— another of Stanley's semantic considerations—would have plagued the Anglo-Saxon poet or his audience any more than we today need unanimity of opinion in our visualization of creatures from our spatial frontier: *eotenas* were larger-than-life land creatures, and *nicoras* amphibious beasts of somewhat horrifying proportions—that is all they needed for the poetic imagination.[22] *Aglœca* and *fyrs* are somewhat different matters, and I shall comment on these in a moment. But first, the translation:

22. Cf. W. K. Wimsatt's remarks on the uses of imprecise relevance in variation, cited in Greenfield (n. 1 above) 62.

"Lord Hrothgar, I am one whose kin and
King is Hylac; as a young warrior
I assayed many mighty deeds. The
Account of Grendel has reached me
At home: travellers tell how this high hall
Stands empty, useless to anyone,
Its brightness dimmed when the light of day
Restward sinks beneath the heaven's vault.
Then my people, those blessed in wisdom,
Conversant with such matters, counselled
Me, King Hrothgar, that I seek you out,
Because they'd proved my craft and power:
They themselves saw me come from combat
Victorious where I vanquished five
And rooted out a race of giants,
Though sore beset slew sea-beasts at night,
Ground down fierce foes seeking destruction,
Righted Weders' wrongs. And now alone
Must I Grendel, mighty opposite,
Blood-thirsting demon, call to account."

While I will not analyze all the effects for which I have striven,
a few further points that Stanley cogently argues might well be
highlighted, since it has been my purpose to prove that more
attention to the esthetics of Old English poetry can contribute
to a better revelation of its meaning. First, I hope I have
obviated the difficulty of *wean ahsodon* by being as imprecise
as the original in my "Ground down fierce foes seeking destruction."[23] (I thus avoid the parentheses or dashes around the
phrase inserted by most editors.) Of greater significance, however, is the *gestalt* of lines 419–26. Stanley has observed a loose
syntax, making for interpretive problems, in lines 419–23; but
this seems to me part of the deliberate esthetic effect of the
passage, stressing the difficulties as well as the accomplish-
ments of the hero. (In this connection *fah*, line 420, taken in

23. Cf. Dudley Fitts, "The Poetic Nuance," *On Translation* (n. 3 above)
46: "[The poetic translator] must be enough of a psychologist and literary
historian to be able to judge whether or not a passage was obscure to begin
with. If it was, it should remain obscure in his translation."

conjunction with *nearoþearfe dreah*, line 422b, probably refers to Beowulf's being bloodied from his *own* wounds.) In contrast to this loose syntax and the suggestion of encounters with *many* foes, there follows the one-on-one contest Beowulf foresees, forcefully expressed in the directness of the triple variation of lines 424b–26a, with its *"wið Grendel, / wið þæm aglæcan, . . . / wið þyrse"*—a progression, it may be noted, from a personalized and named antagonist, to the ambiguous *aglæca* (a term which, as Stanley observes, is applied simultaneously later in the poem to Beowulf and the dragon and thus can hardly be "monster" or "wretch"), to the demonic nature of the fen-inhabiting *þyrs*. My translation tries to capture the complexity of this combination by putting the "I" (Beowulf) cheek by jowl with "Grendel" in the middle of the line (an emphasis frequent across the caesura in the Anglo-Saxon poetic line), and keeping the triple variation by the precise imprecision of "mighty opposite" for *aglæcan* (which not only gives a proper literal meaning for the word, but also captures that sense of Grendel as anti-thane, in opposition to Beowulf, that Irving has exploited[24]), and climaxing in the "blood-thirsting demon" (one who knows the Old English may find the echo of *þyrs* here an added effect). Finally, my translation of these last verses suggests the sense of destinal appointment in its "Must . . . / call to account."

Like Pygmalion, I have fallen in love with my own artistic creations. Whether the gods will be moved to make my translations live for a generation of readers and bear the scrutiny of scholars, I cannot say, but I hope such poetic recreations (and those I may attempt in the future) will at least tempt the non-scholar into learning enough Anglo-Saxon against which to test them on his poetic pulse. But whatever results from these endeavors of mine, I trust that I have convincingly demonstrated that a closer attention to the fusion of esthetics, lexicon, and syntax in Old English poems can lighten the darkness

24. Edward B. Irving, Jr., *A Reading of Beowulf* (New Haven and London 1968) Ch. 3, especially 110–11.

of even difficult portions of them, and thus help close the gap between us and the heart of the Anglo-Saxon poetic experience.[25]

25. Professor Robert P. Creed has kindly read through this essay and made a number of helpful suggestions. In particular he has convinced me that my nine-syllable ideal should not be Procrustean; and he has offered a number of revisions of specific lines, several of which I have silently adopted. The reader might find it interesting to compare my original translation of lines 39-43 of *The Seafarer* with Creed's revised rendering and with my final version (on p. 96 above):

> for there is no man on earth so sea-
> soned in spirit, so proud in fortune,
> so graced in youth, his lord so gracious,
> whose sea-faring causes no concern
> as to what for him the Lord provides;
> > [Greenfield original]
> for there's no man on earth so sea-
> soned in spirit, so sure of fortune,
> so graced by youth and a gracious lord
> that his sea-faring takes no care
> of what the Lord has in store for him.
> > [Creed version]

THE EDITING OF OLD ENGLISH POETIC TEXTS: QUESTIONS OF STYLE

Roy F. Leslie

STYLISTICS HAS NOT HITHERTO played a systematic or important part in the solution of editorial problems in Old English poetry. However, considerations of style may be used to augment linguistic factors in an attempt to produce a text that represents as closely as possible an editor's apprehension of the original work. However diverse their approaches to the editorial task, this has been the aim of most editors; from the eighteenth to the early twentieth century, editors allowed themselves great latitude and thereby brought conjectural emendation into disrepute.[1] This practice was characterized by what George Kane describes as "excessive subjectivity, an identification with the author leading to the assumption that the editor perfectly commanded [the author's] style, or a supersession of author by editor."[2] Such excesses led Eugene

---

1. For a summary of the whole question of "textual criticism," see Leighton D. Reynolds and Nigel G. Wilson, *Scribes and Scholars: A Guide to the Transmission of Latin and Greek Literature* (2nd ed. London 1974) 187ff. A detailed study of the causes of corruption in manuscripts is to be found in James Willis, *Latin Textual Criticism* (Urbana Ill. 1972). See also E. J. Kenney, *The Classical Text* (Berkeley 1974), and the replacement for the third edition of Paul Maas, *Textkritik* (Stuttgart 1957) requested by his publishers from Martin L. West, and published by them in 1973 as *Textual Criticism and Editorial Technique.*

2. George Kane, "Conjectural Emendation," based on a paper read to the Oxford Medieval Society in 1966, was originally published in *Medieval Literature and Civilization: Studies in Memory of G. N. Garmonsway*, ed. Derek A. Pearsall and R. A. Waldron (London 1969) 155–69. It has been

Vinaver to determine, "on strictly objective grounds, what considerations *should* dictate the editor's choice, and how far he is entitled to go in emending his text."[3] He then outlines the mechanisms of scribal transcription, which are capable of producing no fewer than six types of emendable error. He maintains, however, that no matter how strongly an editor may condemn his text on rational grounds, he has to leave it intact at those points at which it is possible that the author, not the scribe, is responsible for it. Vinaver defines the task of the editor as a *partial* reconstruction of the lost original and states that he must aim not at restoring the original work in every particular, but merely at lessening the damage done by the copyists.[4]

In reaction to conjectural emendation, a number of editors of Old English texts had already adopted a conservative attitude toward their texts before the date of Vinaver's article. However, their defense of the authority of Anglo-Saxon scribes had been excessive and had occasioned Kenneth Sisam's inquiry into the accuracy of transmission of Old English poetry;[5] he examines those few poetic texts which occur in more than one manuscript, and concludes that in three of them the tenth-century texts show no attempt to reproduce the archaic or dialectal forms and spellings of the earlier copies. He provides evidence from proper names to demonstrate slipshod copying. He also points out that the difference between a better reading and a worse is a matter of judgment, that to support a bad

---

reprinted in *Medieval Manuscripts and Textual Criticism*, ed. Christopher Kleinhenz, North Carolina Studies in the Romance Languages and Literatures: Symposia, No. 4 (Chapel Hill N.C. 1976) 213 (referred to below as Kleinhenz).

3. Eugene Vinaver, "Principles of Textual Emendation," published originally in *Studies in French Language and Mediaeval Literature: Presented to Professor Mildred K. Pope* (Manchester 1939) 351-69, and reprinted in Kleinhenz, 140.

4. Ibid. (in Kleinhenz) 157.

5. Kenneth Sisam, "The Authority of Old English Poetical Manuscripts," published originally in *Review of English Studies* 22 (1946) 257-68, and reprinted in his *Studies in the History of Old English Literature* (Oxford 1953) 29-44.

manuscript reading is in no way more meritorious than to support a bad conjecture, that a bad manuscript reading, if defended, looks like solid evidence for the defense of other readings. Sisam does, however, also remind us that manuscripts are our primary witnesses.[6]

My own editorial approach is empirical, with a bias in favor of the text, knowing that it may well be unreliable, but aware also that it is the only foundation we have. I am ready to change the text only as a last resort, bearing in mind the temptations that beset an editor to prefer his own readings on insufficient textual evidence. One must agree with Kane when he urges that we be bolder on occasion;[7] however, in editing *Piers Plowman* he had checks and balances that single-text editors do not possess. But an editor of a unique text must be doubly sure that he is being bold with good reason and avoid emendation where the text as it stands makes perfectly good sense. An example of this kind is the manuscript reading *oft* in *The Wanderer* 53, which occurs in a context that is notoriously difficult to interpret; the word is regularly emended to *eft*, "back, again," though it is possible to make sense of the passage using the manuscript form *oft*, "often."[8]

Before we attempt to show, in detail, how stylistics may have a bearing on editorial practices, it is worth noting that the corpus of Old English poetry is small and consists, for the most part, of unique manuscripts which contain many *hapax legomena*. Punctuation is sporadic and, where it does occur, may be used for purposes other than to mark off syntactical units. Word division sometimes appears arbitrary and may obscure meaning. The text is written continuously, like prose, and in any case the verse is in a form unfamiliar to modern readers. For all these reasons, few statements about the literary or the linguistic aspects of a poem can be made with absolute certainty. This is especially true of characteristics of style, which are often difficult to pinpoint and gain agreement on; for although scholars will agree that such things as variation and

6. Ibid. (in *Studies*) 39.
7. Kane (in Kleinhenz, n. 2 above) 225.
8. Roy F. Leslie, ed., *The Wanderer* (Manchester 1966) 76–80.

parallelism exist, they will not always agree about the particular application of them. One critic's variation may be another's parallelism and a third's multiple objects. We therefore do not yet have a clear enough conception of stylistic norms in Old English poetry to make them reliable as criteria for emendation by themselves. What we must do in the meantime is to yoke them with other factors which point in a given direction, or use them as best we can when other factors cancel each other out.

Modern editors have, in fact, yoked literary, if not specifically stylistic evidence, to linguistic factors to an increasing extent. This has given rise to a problem about priorities. For instance, in several places in their edition of *The Wanderer*, Dunning and Bliss suggest that decisions should be made on literary rather than on linguistic grounds.[9] Bruce Mitchell has contested the validity of their proposal, claiming that they have let literary considerations outweigh not linguistic arguments but linguistic facts.[10] For Mitchell, a linguistic fact is "a statement which limits [the editor's] choice of interpretations; for example, that a particular metrical pattern is impossible, that a given inflexional ending is unambiguous, that the word being discussed means 'x' and not 'y', that a conjunction expresses a particular relationship, . . . or that a certain word order is found only in principal clauses."[11] We should certainly not underestimate these constraints within which we must operate, and my own predilection would assuredly not be to make an editorial decision in deliberate defiance of them. However, incontestable linguistic facts are rare and, as they stand in the manuscript, may appear to be incompatible with each other. An editor may, therefore, be forced to emend on semantic or syntactical grounds. His case for emendation is strengthened, however, if a weak and ambiguous passage

9. Thomas P. Dunning and Alan J. Bliss, eds., *The Wanderer* (London 1969) 14, 111 (footnote to line 33).

10. Bruce Mitchell, "Linguistic Facts and the Interpretation of Old English Poetry," *Anglo-Saxon England* 4 (1975) 11–28.

11. Ibid. 11.

becomes a stylistically, as well as linguistically, satisfying one thereby. One such circumstance occurs in *The Wanderer*:

> Swa cwæð eardstapa   earfeþa gemyndig,
> wraþra wælsleahta,   winemæga hryre.[12] (6–7)

We have two unambiguously genitive nouns, *earfeþa* and *wraþra wælsleahta*, dependent on *gemyndig*, which also takes the genitive in all other similar constructions occurring in Old English poetic texts. A third element, the noun phrase *winemæga hryre* (7b), is semantically linked to these two, but it cannot be parallel to them, dependent on *gemyndig*, as one might reasonably expect, because *hryre* is not in the genitive. Nora Kershaw's suggestion that we should read *hryre* as a loose causal or comitative dative, would appear to reconcile these two incompatible linguistic facts.[13] But her suggestion is a counsel of despair, stylistically divorcing the last phrase from its neighbors and providing a weak grammatical explanation.

However, if we emend *hryre* to the genitive *hryres*, we have three parallel expressions whose increasing emotional intensity is reflected by their increasing semantic and grammatical weight, from the simple noun, *earfeþa*, through the modified noun, *wraþra wælsleahta*, to the final phrase, *winemæga hryre*. I believe that we may reasonably posit authorial or scribal error at this point, on two counts. First, there is the remoteness—at the end of the next line—of the phrase from *gemyndig*. Second, the corpus of Old English poetry contains many phrases that consist of a noun in the genitive plus *hryre*, and in these phrases *hryre* is almost invariably in the oblique case. It would appear that the habitual use of the dative formula had led the author or scribe to overlook the necessity here of using the genitive.

I stated above my view that editors should normally emend only as a last resort, but that we should take George Kane's

12. Leslie (n. 8 above) 61. "Thus spoke the wanderer, mindful of hardships, of dreadful massacres, [of] the fall of kinsmen." I believed then that *hryre* could be a genitive. I now feel that the form should be *hryres*.

13. Nora Kershaw, *Anglo-Saxon and Norse Poems* (Cambridge 1922) notes to lines 6–7.

advice and be bolder on occasion. A case in point is a passage in *The Seafarer*, where the decision to emend the unique compound *cearselda* (5b) may be made largely on stylistic grounds:

> siþas secgan,   hu ic geswincdagum
> earfoðhwile   oft þrowade
> bitre breostceare   gebiden hæbbe
> gecunnad in ceole   cearselda fela.[14] (2-5)

One must balance the fact that some kind of sense can be made of the word as it stands, with the improvement in clarity of meaning that follows from the simplest of emendations that can be made to an Old English word, namely the alteration of *d* to *ð*.

Cearselda is usually translated "abodes of care / suffering / sorrow." Ida L. Gordon refers to *meduseld*, "mead-hall," (*Beowulf* 3065) as a parallel;[15] but *meduseld* is not a true parallel, for the first element refers to "mead" and not to an abstract concept such as "grief," as it does in the closer parallel, *dreorsele*, "desolate hall" (*The Wife's Lament* 50). There are, however, semantic difficulties with the verb *cunnian*, "to experience," which, in marine contexts, always refers to the sea itself, not to what is on it, as in *The Seafarer: þæt ic hean streamas / sealtyþa gelac sylf cunnige*, "so that I myself should experience the tumult of the waves" (34-35); or in the closer parallel to this particular passage in *Andreas*:

> Swa gesælde iu,   þæt we on sæbate
> ofer waruðgewinn   wæda cunnedan.[16] (438-40)

On the other hand, if we make the emendation of *d* to *ð*, to give *cearsēlða*, with a long *ē* in the second syllable, we have the Anglian equivalent of West-Saxon *cearsǣlða*, which would

14. "relate my journeys, how I in days of toil often suffered times of hardship, have experienced bitter breast-care, had many abodes/experiences of care on a ship." For the text see Ida L. Gordon, ed., *The Seafarer* (London 1960) 33.

15. Ibid. 33 *n*.

16. "So it happened long ago, that we tested the waves over the tumult of the surf on a ship." For the text see George P. Krapp, ed., *The Vercelli Book, The Anglo-Saxon Poetic Records* (hereafter *ASPR*) 2 (New York 1932) 15.

mean "experiences of care." Although this compound does not occur elsewhere, we may note that *heardsǣlþ*, "hard fate," "misfortune," is listed in Bosworth-Toller, and note also the occurrence of *earfoðsǣlig* "unblessed," *heardsǣlig* "unfortunate," and *wansǣlig* "miserable," "evil." If we adopt *cearsēlða* in the *Seafarer* passage, we find ourselves with two interwoven patterns of three variants each, one of verbal expressions on the theme of endurance (*þrowade*, *gebiden hæbbe* and *gecunnad*), and one of nominal expressions on the theme of times of anxiety (*geswincdagum*, *earfoðhwīle* and *cearsēlða*). We then have a passage strikingly similar in impact to *Deor*:

> Welund him be wurman wræces cunnade,
> anhydig eorl earfoþa dreag,
> hæfde him to gesiþþe sorge ond longaþ.[17] (1-3)

So far I have shown how considerations of style can come to the aid of an editor in elucidating meaning in individual phrases. I turn now to the wider topic of punctuation, where editorial practice can have a marked effect on our apprehension of both the meaning and the style of a poem. Because of the sporadic nature of manuscript punctuation, and our imperfect understanding of its application, editors have nearly always added modern punctuation to their texts. Mostly they have ignored the manuscript punctuation, but recent editors have sometimes sought to explain and incorporate it.

How punctuation affects style can be illustrated with a passage from *The Seafarer*, which deals with bird cries as substitutes for various human pleasures:

> Þær ic ne gehyrde butan hlimman sæ
> iscaldne wæg hwilum ylfete song
> dyde ic me to gomene ganetes hleoþor
> ond huilpan sweg fore hleahtor wera
> mæw singende fore medodrince. (18-22)

The scheme of punctuation that we impose on this passage

17. "Weland had for himself experience of persecution by the sword, the resolute nobleman, suffered hardships, had for his company sorrow and longing." For the text see *ASPR* 3 (New York 1936) 178.

affects the pattern of variation. Among recent editors, both Krapp and Dobbie[18] and Ida L. Gordon make lines 19b–22 a complete sentence, which may be translated "At times the song of the swan I took for my pleasure, the cry of the gannet and the sound of the curlew for the laughter of men, the sea-gull crying for the drinking of mead." Mrs. Gordon points out that these lines modify the statement (18–19a) that nothing could be heard but the roaring of the sea; however, instead of linking them in one sentence, she concludes that more proba-bly the change of sense and construction comes, as so often in Old English poetry, in the middle of the line, and she therefore begins a new sentence with *hwilum* in the middle of line 19.

A second pattern is produced by a modification of the above. As before, *hwilum* begins a new sentence which is, however, modified internally, by a comma after *hleoþor* at the end of line 20. The speaker then has both the swan's song *and* the gannet's cry for his pleasure, followed by the curlew's cry for the laughter of men (21) and the seagull singing for the drinking of mead (22).

A case can be made for quite another pattern of punctua-tion. If we place a stop after *song* at the end of line 19, *ylfete song* becomes an additional object of *gehyrde* (18) in the first sentence, and we have a one-to-one correspondence in the second: the cry of the gannet for pleasure, the curlew's call for the laughter of men, and the gull singing for the mead-drink-ing. My own preference is for this version because it is more balanced and because it conforms with the only punctuation point, after *song*, on the whole manuscript page (folio 81b).

Donald Fry's punctuation in his recent revision of part of the Finnsburg episode in *Beowulf* departs markedly from the generally accepted practice:

> Gewiton him ða wigend   wica neosian
> freondum befeallen,   Frysland geseon.
> Hamas ond hea-burh   Hengest ða gyt
> wæl-fagne winter   wunode mid Finne
> *ea*l unhlitme   (eard gemunde),

18. Ibid. 35.

þeah þe he meahte   on mere drifan
hringed-stefnan.   (1125–31)[19]

It has been customary to put full stops, or semicolons, after *heaburh* (1127) and *unhlitme* (1129) to give a translation such as the following: "Then Finn's fighting men, bereft of their friends, departed to make their way to their own abodes and see the land of the Frisians, their homes and their lofty stronghold. But Hengest still dwelt with Finn throughout that slaughter-stained winter—most unhappy was his lot. He remembered his homeland, although he could not put out to sea in his ship with the curling prow."[20] The word "not" in this last sentence is the result of the emendation of *he* to *ne*; Fry retains the manuscript *he*, and puts no punctuation after *heaburh* and *unhlitme*, but puts a stop after *geseon* (1126), a comma at the end of 1129, and parentheses round the phrase *eard gemunde*. He translates lines 1127–31 as follows: "yet Hengest, during the slaughter-stained winter, inhabited with Finn the houses and the high-fortress *eal unhlitme* ["voluntarily": Fry, p. 22] (he thought of home), although he could drive the ring-prowed ship over the sea."[21] Here I am primarily concerned with his abstraction of the phrase *Hamas ond hea-burh* (1127) from its syntactical relationship with the sentence in the preceding lines and his use of it to begin a new sentence, not as a subject, but as the object of *wunode* (1128). Now we cannot rule out this procedure on idiomatic grounds, because *wunode* can take a direct object; however, we would expect inversion of subject and verb after an initial object of the weight of *Hamas ond hea-burh*, so that *wunode* would be followed by *Hengest*. Moreover, the change in punctuation here destroys the eminently satisfactory stylistic relationship with the previous two lines, wherein we have a pleasing arrangement, with *Hamas* echoing *wica*, and both *Hamas* and *hea-burh* reflecting the scope of the survey of Frisia.

19. Donald K. Fry, ed., *Finnsburh: Fragment and Episode* (London 1974) 42–43; Introduction 20–22.

20. Translated by George N. Garmonsway and Jacqueline Simpson, *Beowulf and its Analogues* (London 1968) 31.

21. Fry (n. 19 above) 21.

The use of capitals in Old English poetic texts varies widely, even within the same manuscript. In the introduction to their edition of *The Exeter Book*, Krapp and Dobbie give a list of the capitals in each poem.[22] They vary in frequency of occurrence from about one in every 3½ lines in *Guthlac*, to one in almost 11 lines in *Christ*. Shorter but similar poems can have an equally wide variation; *The Seafarer* with 124 lines has only six altogether, whereas *The Wanderer*, with 115 lines, has twice as many. In consequence, editors have placed little reliance on them hitherto. Therefore, a great deal of interest was aroused when Dunning and Bliss suggested that the small capitals in *The Wanderer* appear to be designed to mark out independent sections in the progression of the poem.[23] Many of them in fact do correspond with divisions that have been made by scholars on syntactical and other grounds. They occur at the beginning of lines 6 and 8, marking off the two lines concerning the *eardstapa* himself as in some way parenthetic; at the beginning of the wanderer's general reflections at line 58; at the start of the impersonal elegiac passage at line 73; and to mark out what I have interpreted as the limits to the *ubi sunt* passage (88–96).

Some of the capitals put forward have been disputed, on the basis that they are too small, or at best ambiguous;[24] for, in a number of Old English letters, the capital is simply a larger form of the lower case letter. I am, therefore, confining my attention to the undisputed ones. Do they go back to the author, or are they to be attributed to a scribe—either the copyist of *The Exeter Book* or a predecessor? If they are scribal in origin, how reliable are they? The scribe may occasionally have been in error about the structure of the poem he was transcribing. In the following passage from *The Wanderer*, this may well have happened:

> Forþon wat se þe sceal   his winedryhtnes
> leofes larcwidum   longe forþolian

22. *ASPR* 3, lxxvi–lxxxi.
23. Dunning and Bliss (n. 9 above) 4–7.
24. See review of Dunning and Bliss by Stanley B. Greenfield in *Notes and Queries* 215 (1970) 115.

ðonne sorg ond slæp   somod ætgædre
earmne anhogan   oft gebindað·
þinceð him on mode   þæt he his mondryhten
clyppe ond cysse   ond on cneo lecge
honda ond heafod   swa he hwilum ær
in geardagum   giefstolas breac
ðonne onwæcneð eft   wineleas guma
gesihð him biforan   fealwe wegas
baþian brimfuglas   brædan feþra
hreosan hrim ond snaw   hægle gemenged.[25] (37–48)

Perhaps the scribe has mistakenly capitalized the wrong *ðonne* in one or more of a series of four: *ðõn* (small cap *ð*) in lines 39 and 45, and *þõn* (lower case *þ*) in lines 49 and 51. Dunning and Bliss depart from their adherence to the manuscript capitalization as guidance to the beginnings of new sentences, by making *þonne* in line 49 begin a new sentence, and by correlating it with *þonne* at beginning of line 51.[26] On the face of it, the two correlations of the four *ðonne* / *þonne* clauses are stylistically attractive, as is the editors' claim that the first grouping gives an effective picture of fitful slumber. But there are consequential problems, particularly with respect to the preceding lines, 37 and 38, which are left in isolation, without an easily discernible object for the verb *wat* (37). Dunning and Bliss put forward three reasons for denying this verb its traditional object, the noun clause *þinceð him on mode* (41). The first is admittedly that it does not fit their explanation of the syntactical implications of the four *ðonnes*. The second arises from their belief that the traditional punctuation produces a substantial anti-climax, and is of course a subjective assessment. Their third objection would appear at first sight to have

25. "Therefore he knows the one who has had long to forgo the counsel of his dear lord how when sorrow and sleep both together often bind the wretched solitary one it seems to him in his mind that he embraces and kisses his liege lord and on his knee lays his hands and head as he at times before in days gone by had enjoyed the throne then the friendless man awakes again sees before him the fallow waves the sea-birds bathing spreading their feathers he sees the frost and snow falling mixed with hail." For the text see Leslie (n. 8 above) 62 (caps. and punct. omitted).

26. Dunning and Bliss (n. 9 above) 21.

more substance. They suggest that the use of the noun object *earmne anhogan* (40) in the subsidiary clause is unidiomatic, since normal usage would place a qualification in the principal clause, with a pronoun object in the subordinate clause. But the poet has in fact already departed from normal usage by putting the *ðonne* clause first. He may have done so advisedly, to get the description of the impact of sorrow and sleep out of the way first so that he could make an uninterrupted sweep through the vivid dreams that peak in the climactic ceremony before the throne that the wanderer enjoyed in former days, a ceremony whose importance to the heroic literary tradition can hardly be overestimated.

Manuscript word division presents the editor with many difficulties, for word elements and short words do not conform to modern practices in this matter. Moreover, the elements of compounds are almost always written as separate words. For example, the opening line of *The Seafarer* appears as: *Mæg ic beme sylfum soð gied wrecan* in the manuscript, and is usually rendered in modern texts as: *mæg ic be me sylfum soðgied wrecan*, "I can utter a true tale about myself."

Many elements may be linked with confidence to form compound words, often because the context is unambiguous, and the proposed first element lacks any inflection which would force us to consider it as a separate word. For example, *medo* and *drince*, and *stan* and *clifu* in *The Seafarer* folio 81b, line 15, may be linked to form compounds, but not *ganetes* and *hleoþor* (fol. 81b lines 13–14), because of the genitive singular ending of *ganetes*.

Where we have an uninflected adjective followed by a noun, ambiguity may result; we then have the option of leaving the words separate or joining them to make a compound. The decision has to be made with the help of contextual clues. In the opening section of *The Wanderer* several such decisions have to be made, for example, concerning *werig* and *mod* (15), and *hreo* and *hyge* (16). Dunning and Bliss make the point that editors who join *werig* and *mod* should also join *hreo* and *hyge*, because of the obvious parallelism between the two lines:

Ne mæg werig mod   wyrde wiðstondan,
ne se hreo hyge   helpe gefremman.[27] (15–16)

In my edition I had destroyed the parallelism between them by reading *werigmod* (15) and *hreo hyge* (16). I concede that there are no compelling linguistic or structural reasons for making the former a compound, and am glad to restore the parallelism by concurring in the Dunning and Bliss reading of *werig* and *mod* as separate words.

There is a similar situation in *The Wanderer*, with the unique sequences of *winter* and *cearig* (24) and *sele* and *dreorig* (25):

wod wintercearig   ofer waþe[m]a gebind,
sohte seledreorig   sinces bryttan.[28] (24–25)

As a compound, *wintercearig* has two possible meanings, "worn with winter cares" or, "worn with the cares of age" (of "many winters"), either of which would fit the context well. The interpretation of the relationship between *sele* and *dreorig* is another matter. Did the wanderer, sad, seek the hall of a giver of treasure? Or, hall-sad (that is, sad at the loss of the hall company), did he seek a giver of treasure? The latter reading is probably the more acceptable one in Old English and gives a compound which can be looked upon as an echo of *wintercearig* in the previous line.

Sele occurs again, in line 34: *Gemon he selesecgas ond sincþege*, "he remembers hall-retainers and the receiving of treasure." Parallels such as the undisputed compounds, *seleþegn*, "hall-thane" (1794) and *seldguma*, "hall-man" (249) in *Beowulf* justify a compound *selesecgas*. The *Beowulf* contexts indicate retainers of a rather lowly status, the servants in the hall, rather than the warriors' peers, and we can infer a similar meaning for *selesecgas*. As a compound it would appear to be supported stylistically by its balance with *sincþege*. If we do not read it as a compound we weaken the

27. "Nor can the weary spirit withstand fate, nor the troubled breast afford help." Ibid. 107.
28. Leslie (n. 8 above) 61; see 70 for commentary.

dramatic impact of the lines by having the wanderer remember "the hall, the men and the gift-receiving." The first and the last memory are connected, but *secgas*, which by itself has no connection with the hall or any of its ceremonies, is there like the unwanted guest at a party. Moreover, the balance of the line is destroyed. It is structurally a self-contained unit and needs internal balance. The *hu* clause that follows is like *selesecgas* and *sincþege*, dependent on *gemon*, but remains structurally distinct.

The Wife's Lament, Het mec hlaford min her heard niman (15), is difficult to interpret, whether we read *her heard* as two separate words or as a compound.[29] Some scholars have taken *heard*, "stern," as an adjective modifying *hlaford*, "lord," but to have a noun separated from its modifier by a possessive pronoun and an adverb is unidiomatic. Moreover, if we read *her* and *heard* as separate words, we have a metrically defective line with double alliteration in the second half. If we combine the two words, we have not only a unique compound, but one that has no parallels in Old English literature. Emendation of *heard* to *eard* can be justified by postulating accidental repetition of *h* from the previous word, and produces the idiomatic expression *eard niman* "to take up residence." Basically we have to make a decision as to whether we have two separate words or one compound. The reflection of the phrase, *her heard niman* in *on þissum londstede*, "in this country" (16b), appears to me to be a factor to be added to the other considerations discussed, in favor, not only of retaining separate words, but of the emendation of *heard* to *eard*.

As may be deduced from the foregoing analyses, the ideal editor should be part literary critic and part philologist. He has considerable powers to influence our understanding of a poem, and considerable opportunities to abuse that power. The critic in him may succumb to the temptation to come to the text with a ready-made theory about its style and meaning, and thus see only that evidence which fits his theory. That almost any theory can be made to fit a poem can be seen from the spectrum of critical assessment of *The Wanderer* and *The*

29. Roy F. Leslie, ed., *Three Old English Elegies* (Manchester 1961) 47.

Seafarer, which has ranged from seeing them as simple sea poems, through elegiac lyrics, to allegories of recondite Christian doctrine.

The philologist in the editor makes him examine small contexts in great detail. He is apt to take, and indeed should take, a worm's-eye view of the poem, submitting himself to the discipline involved in the close scrutiny of small units. By working outwards from a narrow context he may perceive what others overlook; he will be less tempted to generalize on the basis of insufficient evidence. But he must also be aware of the danger of dealing in unrelated fragments. Kenneth Sisam warned us that intensive study of a text with a strong bias towards the manuscript reading may blunt the sense of style.[30] But if we are too confident in our pronouncements on style, without due regard to our limited knowledge, we will return to the excessively subjective judgments of a former age.

Even if our knowledge of Old English poetic patterns were to increase greatly, E. G. Stanley's doubts would remain valid,[31] and we may always have to content ourselves with looking through a glass darkly. However, intensive and thorough surveys, made possible by modern technology, may go some way toward compensating us for the small volume of the literature available to us. These would include the Old English dictionary, a KWIC concordance for the whole body of Old English poetry, Bruce Mitchell's volume on Old English syntax, and other specialized studies, such as Hans Schabram's books on *Superbia*,[32] on particular concepts and specific areas of the Old English vocabulary.

30. Sisam, in *Studies* (n. 5 above) 39.
31. See E. G. Stanley's paper in this volume.
32. Hans Schabram, *Superbia* I (Munich 1965).

TWO ASPECTS OF VARIATION IN
OLD ENGLISH POETRY

Fred C. Robinson

D ISCUSSION OF OLD ENGLISH stylistic devices is problematic from the outset, for we have no contemporary treatises on style to aid us in establishing historically valid definitions. There is no *Ars poetica* of Old English verse; there is not even a *Skáldskaparmál*. The technique of *variation* is a case in point.[1] Since the term has no authority in Anglo-Saxon tradition but is an invention pure and simple of modern scholarship, any definition offered now by a student of Old English poetry must be regarded as little more than stipulative.[2] I claim no more than this for the definition I set out below, although I have tried to include within it those features which most scholars have associated with the term, and I have contrived to gain some small status for my definition by locating it briefly within the mainstream of scholarly debate on variation since the term was introduced in the nineteenth century. If I appear to pass hurriedly and selectively through the accumulated commentary on the nature of the figure, it is

1. The phrase *wordum wrixlan* in *Beowulf* 874 has been interpreted by some scholars as a contemporary allusion to the technique of variation, but since *wordum wrixlan* occurs elsewhere with the unambiguous meaning "to speak, converse," a meaning which yields acceptable sense in *Beowulf* 874, this isolated occurrence would seem insufficient evidence for the technical sense. Cf. German *Wortwechsel* "discussion, dispute."

2. Consequently, any dispute over which scholar's definition of the figure is "right" is meaningless. My own definition excludes Roy F. Leslie's "conceptual variation" and Kemp Malone's "outer variation," for I do not find these usages helpful; but their formulations are no less "right" than my own.

because my primary concern in this essay is not with definition *per se* but rather with scrutinizing two of the generally recognized types of variation in order to deepen in some small measure our understanding of how Old English poets used this stylistic device.

When John Milton described the style of the Old English poem *Brunanburh*, contrasting it with the style of the surrounding prose of the *Chronicle*, he chose the term "over-charg'd" to characterize the poetry.[3] Since his paraphrase of *Brunanburh* "in usuall language" tends to excise the frequent restatements in the poem, it seems likely that "over-charg'd" refers to those carefully massed tautologies which later critics would denominate *variation*. Similar comments were made by other early readers of Old English, but little can be made of these observations. They prove only that the characteristic restatements of Old English poems are a prominent feature which cannot fail to attract the attention of even the most casual observer.[4]

"A strong tendency toward apposition" is the way Henry Sweet described Old English poetic style in 1870,[5] and here we move toward a more precise characterization of variation. But "apposition" is not quite adequate to describe poetic restatements which involve not only nouns and pronouns, but also verbs, adjectives, phrases, and even entire sentences. Recognizing the need for a special term, Richard Heinzel, in 1875, introduced the word *Variation* to describe the phenomenon.[6]

3. *Complete Prose Works of John Milton*, ed. Don M. Wolfe (New Haven 1953-   ) 5.308–09. Milton would have read the Old English poem in the edition of Abraham Wheloc, relying heavily, no doubt, on the Latin translation provided therein.

4. Thus Sharon Turner gave some attention to "the repetition of synonymous expressions" in *The History of the Anglo-Saxons* 3 (4th ed. 3 vols. London 1823) 258–65, as did John J. Conybeare in his *Illustrations of Anglo-Saxon Poetry* (London 1826) xxviii–xxxii and 6; see Calder's essay above 8.

5. Henry Sweet, "Sketch of the History of Anglo-Saxon Poetry" in W. Carew Hazlitt's edition of Thomas Warton's *History of English Poetry from the Twelfth to the Close of the Sixteenth Century* 2 (4 vols. London 1871) 5.

6. Richard Heinzel, *Über den Stil der altgermanischen Poesie* (Strasbourg 1875) 3–9, 49.

His definition was somewhat vague, however, and subsequent scholars such as Rudolf Kögel and Paul Pachaly[7] blurred the concept further when they explained Heinzel's term as a loose metaphor derived from musical composition—theme and variation. The original statement of a concept or referent would be the theme, presumably, and subsequent appositional restatements would be the variations. But this metaphorical interpretation of the term seems fanciful. Heinzel, I feel certain, was adopting a Latin rhetorical term (although he does not say so) and applying it to Germanic poetry. The term appears to have been developed for the most part by post-Classical writers; one finds a typical use, with definition, in the *Carmen de figuris vel schematibus* edited by Karl Halm in 1863.[8] James Henry coins the term anew in his edition of the *Aeneid* published two years before Heinzel's treatise,[9] and *Variation* was also popular among German writers on prose style in the eighteenth century. That the word was from the beginning a technical rhetorical term is a point worth establishing, for the alternative assumption of a musical metaphor underlying the concept *variation* can only serve to impede clear definition of the term.

My own definition, which is a respectful modification of that proposed by Walther Paetzel in his treatise *Die Variationen in der altgermanischen Allitterationspoesie* (Berlin 1913), is as follows: "syntactically parallel words or word-groups which share a common referent and which occur within a single clause (or, in the instance of sentence-variation, within contiguous clauses)." Simply stated, I regard variation as apposition (Sweet's old term), if apposition be extended to include restatements of adjectives, verbs, and phrases as well as of nouns and pronouns. This definition is objective and formal and, as a result, somewhat narrow. Some would complain that it excludes too many collocations that share certain

---

7. Rudolf Kögel, *Geschichte der deutschen Litteratur bis zum Ausgange des Mittelalters* (Strasbourg 1894) 334; Paul Pachaly, *Die Variation im Heliand und in der altsächsischen Genesis* (Jena 1899) 2.

8. Karl F. von Halm, ed., *Rhetores latini minores* (Leipzig 1863) 67, 70.

9. James Henry, ed., *Æneidea* 1 (4 vols. Leipzig 1873–89) 745–51.

qualities with the phenomena I do include.[10] To this objection I would answer that I do not deny that variations strictly defined share fundamental characteristics with other elements of diction and narrative. But I find it more useful not to declare every similar element a variation but rather to recognize that there are some common features shared by stylistic devices which bear different names.

The stylistic functions of variation in Old English poetry are manifold. A cluster of variations can prolong dramatically a crucial moment in a poem. A single variation can effect a swift rhetorical transition without the interrupting mechanics of hypotactic linkage. Variations can register subtle shifts in perspective, a function which Stanley Greenfield has described with particular skill.[11] Variation can introduce rhetorical suspense into a sentence through its effect of artful retardation. And in the best poetry it achieves these effects while simultaneously and effortlessly fulfilling the metrical and alliterative requirements of the verse form. If there were time and space, I should like to examine and admire a selection of variations illustrating each of these functions, but, as it is, I shall deal with only two types, hoping thereby both to sharpen our understanding of the figure and to illustrate how the larger strategies of Old English poetic style sometimes reflect the local tactics of variation.

In the first type of variation to which I shall turn, a referent is designated at least once in literal terms and once by a figurative expression which might be mystifying were it not for the clarification provided by the second, unmetaphorical element. Consider, for example, *Beowulf* 1368-69:

> Ðeah þe *hæðstapa*   hundum geswenced,
> *heorot hornum trum,   holtwudu sece*[12]

10. Ewald Standop is especially skillful in demonstrating the close interrelationship between a wide variety of stylistic devices which he includes under the term *Variation*; see his "Formen der Variation im *Beowulf*," *Festschrift für Edgar Mertner*, ed. Bernhard Fabian and Ulrich Suerbaum (Munich 1969) 55–63.

11. Stanley B. Greenfield, *The Interpretation of Old English Poems* (London and Boston 1972) 68–72.

12. "Although the heath-stalker, pressed by the dogs, the hart strong in

The "heath-stalker" (*hæðstapa*) could be a wolf, or a man, or even a grasshopper, since the compound refers to a single vivid action characteristic of all these creatures. The specifying variation *heorot hornum trum* resolves the synecdochic ambiguity. A similar effect may be seen in *Beowulf* 1745–47:

> þonne bið on hreþre   under helm drepen
> *biteran stræle*   (him bebeorgan ne con),
> *wom wundorbebodum   wergan gastes*[13]

In this highly metaphorical passage from Hrothgar's sermon, clarifying variations repeatedly help the audience through the quasi-allegorical language, explaining that the *weard* of line 1741 is *saweles hyrde*, and so forth. In the passage before us, the symbolic meaning of the metaphorical arrow is spelled out in detail.

A slightly subtler example is the variation in *Beowulf* 1143–44:

> þonne him Hunlafing   *hildeleoman*,
> *billa selest*,   on bearm dyde[14]

Here the ambiguous metaphor *hildeleoman* is clarified by the variation following. Some learned readers of Old English might question whether there really is any ambiguity to be clarified, since swords are frequently spoken of as flames or flashes of battle (*Swurdleoma stod, swylce eal Finnsburuh fyrenu wære* will come to many readers' minds). But the text of *Beowulf* itself shows us that the literal meaning of *hildeleoma* was still very much alive, and hence the epithet *was* ambiguous. For lines 2582–83 contain the same compound used literally to refer to fire:

>   wearp wælfyre;   wide sprungon
> *heldeleoman*[15]

---

horns, should seek the forest." All quotations in this essay are, unless otherwise identified, from George P. Krapp and Elliott V. K. Dobbie, eds., *The Anglo-Saxon Poetic Records* (6 vols. New York 1931–53).

13. "Then he is struck in his heart beneath his helmet with a sharp arrow —he knows not how to protect himself—with the crooked mysterious urgings of the evil spirit."

14. "Whenever the son of Hunlaf placed the battle-flame on his lap, the best of swords."

15. "[The dragon] threw forth deadly fire; the hostile flames leapt far and wide."

Thus the specifying, clarifying variation in lines 1143–44 is not otiose.

Another example raises the old question as to how much dictional skill we can expect from an Old English poet. We have just seen that in *Beowulf* 1143 the root meaning of *hildeleoma* is intact, and thus the word has authentic figurative force. And yet, when we see the same figurative term used of a word in the following passage (*Beowulf* 1522–24), the poet seems to treat the epithet as a dead metaphor, for he combines the flame figure with imagery of biting or eating:

> Ða se gist onfand
> þæt se *beadoleoma*   bitan nolde,
> aldre sceþðan,   ac seo ecg geswac[16]

A doctrinaire oral-formulaist would crow with delight over such an apparent lapse of attention as this, for line 1523 would seem to argue that the poets were too hurried in their composition to notice the literal meanings of their formulas. But we cannot be sure that this is the case. For in an earlier passage where he spoke of the sword's hostile bite on an enemy's body, the poet artfully combines this image with fire-imagery which also involves biting, or at least devouring. The context is the funeral scene in the Finnsburg episode (*Beowulf* 1121–24):

> ðonne blod ætspranc,
> laðbite lices.   *Lig* ealle forswealg,
> *gæsta gifrost*,   þara ðe þær guð fornam
> bega folces[17]

Is it possible, then, that *Beowulf* 1523 involves a *double metaphor*, one prepared for by an earlier variation in which the image of fire as a ravenous devourer is joined with a metaphor of a sword's biting? If so, then in *beadoleoma bitan* we have two bold metaphors resolved harmoniously into one through the agency of the common term *bitan*.

16. "Then the stranger discovered that the battle-flame would not bite, injure the vitals, but the blade failed."

17. "The blood spurted forth from the body's hostile bite. Fire, the greediest of creatures, devoured all of those of the two armies whom war had destroyed there."

Before answering this question in the affirmative, the cautious critic, mindful of E. G. Stanley's masterly demonstration that little is knowable and nothing is certain in the study of Old English style,[18] should pause and ask himself whether he is perhaps reading conscious artistry into a happy accident of traditional poetic diction. I have paused long over this instance, but what prompts me after all to grant the poet at least the possibility of conscious design here is, on the one hand, the superior sensitivity with which he uses traditional diction throughout *Beowulf*, and, on the other, the particular care with which he seems to use fire-imagery in the poem. From the opening prelude where we are told that the house Heorot stands in wait of the hostile fervor of destroying fire until the end where fire is awakened one last time to destroy the *banhus* of the hero's body, the poet seems attentive and deft in his frequent use of fire-imagery. When Grendel makes his last raid on Heorot, for example, we are surprised to hear that the hall stands *fyrbendum fœst* (line 722) "secure in the bonds of fire" only shortly after we were told that hostile fire would destroy the hall (and my own surprise is not entirely allayed by the editors' footnotes assuring us that the reference is to "fire-forged metal braces" or the like). And lest we rush unheeding past this curious description of the fire-doomed hall, the poet introduces at this point, in obvious proximity with *fyrbendum fœst*, a striking simile: Grendel's eyes, as he fixes his gaze on the warrior he will seize and devour, are *ligge gelicost* (line 727) "most like to fire." I find it difficult not to believe, then, that *fyrbendum fœst* carries a discreet but powerful irony. Or again, when, in his speech of advice to Beowulf, Hrothgar enumerates the various ways men may die, one of which, he says, will end Beowulf's life, are we being over-subtle to notice it is the *fyres feng* that actually does destroy Beowulf, and to savor the sad irony that fire's *feng*—its "grip"—will prove greater even than the mighty grip of the hero?

The hostile fire that seizes, bites, and devours throughout the poem seems to me a consistently portrayed, living entity in

18. See Stanley's essay in this volume.

Beowulf—one might almost say a character in the narrative. Its portrayal and meaning are even more consistent than is that of the fire-imagery in Homer, a subject which has been discussed so well and at such length in Cedric Whitman's *Homer and the Heroic Tradition*.[19] And because I am so impressed by the deftness with which the *Beowulf* poet uses fire imagery, I am susceptible to persuasion that the last two passages quoted above may be related and meaningful, rather than a thoughtless bungle.

Turning to another group of "clarifying" variations, a group dealing with warrior bands, I would first call attention to *Exodus* 180–82:

> Ymb hine wægon   *wigend unforhte*,
> *hare heorowulfas*   hilde gretton,
> þurstige þræcwiges,   þeodenholde[20]

Here the literally denominated warriors are characterized further with the somewhat metaphorical variation describing them as wolves. A similar but more problematic example occurs in *Beowulf* 1829–35, where Beowulf vows twice to Hrothgar that he will bring an army to his assistance if need should befall. He says,

> ic ðe þusenda   *þegna* bringe,
> *hæleþa* to helpe . . .
> . . . ic þe wel herige
> ond þe to geoce   *garholt* bere,
> *mægenes fultum*,   þær ðe bið manna þearf[21]

19. Cedric H. Whitman, *Homer and the Heroic Tradition* (Cambridge Mass. 1958) 128–45. Whereas Whitman finds references to fire in the *Iliad* forming a "pattern of associations, all centering around the theme of heroic passion and death (129)," the *Beowulf* poet seems to make the symbolism even more explicit: the heroes of the Old English poem seem always to be pitted against a fire-like inimicality (e.g., the fiery-eyed Grendel who dwells in a fire-lit cave beneath a mere on which burns a supernatural fire, a fiery dragon, the fire that consumes the two royal halls in the poem, the dark fires of the funeral pyre, and the fires of hell).

20. "Around him moved fearless warriors, grey, deadly wolves; loyal to their prince and thirsting for battle, they welcomed war."

21. "I shall bring to your aid a thousand thanes, heroes . . .; I shall honor you [*or* provide you with an army?] and bring to your aid a wooden spear, the support of an army, if you have need of men."

I have always thought there was a touch of bathos in Beowulf's promise to bring along a wooden spear with the multitudes of warriors he will lead to Denmark, and Klaeber too was troubled, asking with an uncertain query whether *garholt* is perhaps a plural and should be rendered "wooden spears," an improvement which seems somehow not to solve the problem. Some may well wonder why this passage is included at all among a list of variations purporting to contain a figurative expression explicated by a literal term.

The answer is that I do take *garholt* as a figurative term: I believe that the baseword *holt* may not mean "wood" in the sense of "material" but "wood" in the sense of "forest." Beowulf, I suggest, is saying, "I shall bring to your support a *forest* of spears!"[22] I make this suggestion not merely because it seems to me to improve the tone and sense of the passage, but also because the metaphor comparing a spear-bearing army to a forest is a traditional trope, one occurring, for example, in line 47 of the Latin version of the *Waldere* legend, where the subject is Attila's army:

Ferrea silva micat totos rutilando per agros[23]
"A forest of iron glistens, gleaming red through all the fields"

Behind this, of course, are references to cornfields of spears and acres of bristling iron in the *Aeneid* and other Latin writings.[24] Lucan (a favorite of Aldhelm's) refers to a warrior with a hyperbolic "forest of spears" in his breast, and William of Malmesbury works this turn of phrase into his account of the wars with Penda.[25] Looking to the Germanic side, we see that

22. Professor Caroline Brady has kindly called my attention to the fact that my interpretation of *garholt* was anticipated by Arthur G. Brodeur in *The Art of Beowulf* (Berkeley 1959) 30. See also Phyllis Hodgson's review of Brodeur in *Modern Language Review* 55 (1960) 426, and Professor Brady's study, "Weapons in *Beowulf*: An Analysis of the Nominal Compounds and an Evaluation of the Poet's Use of Them," forthcoming in *Anglo-Saxon England*.

23. See Karl Strecker's edition of *Waltharius* in *MGH: Poetarum Latinorum Medii Aevi* 6 no. 1, 26.

24. Strecker cites *Aeneid* 11, lines 601–02 and 3, lines 45–46.

25. *Willelmi Malmesbiriensis Monachi: De Gestis Regum Anglorum*, ed. William Stubbs, 1 (2 vols. London 1887–89) 52. Cf. Lucan, *Pharsalia* 6, 205.

the later tradition of the Icelanders has an entire system of
kennings based on warriors imagined as trees: *hildimeiðr*,
vighlynr, geira viðr, and so on. The same image is used, if I am
not mistaken, elsewhere in Old English poetry. *Exodus* 155–59
describes the advance of Pharoah's host in these terms:

> siððan hie gesawon   of suðwegum
> *fyrd* Faraonis   forð ongangan,
> *oferholt* wegan,   *eored* lixan,
> (garas trymedon,   guð hwearfode,
> blicon bordhreoðan,   byman sungon),[26]

where the thickly arrayed spears are pictured as "an over-
whelming forest" (*oferholt*). Actually, my reading of this passage was anticipated by the Bosworth-Toller *Dictionary*, where
we find entered with queries the suggestion that the word *oferholt* might possibly be read here as "a forest of spears which
rise over the heads of those who bear them." This reading has
found little favor with recent editors, who apparently feel that
to translate the simple element *ofer-* as "over the heads of
those who bear them" is supplying a little more than the bare
prefix warrants. I would suggest, however, we need only take
the prefix in the sense which it clearly has in this sentence from
a confessional manual detailing the penalty for rape: "Gyf
hwa mid his *ofercræfte* wif oððe mæden neadinga nymð to
unrihthæmede hire unwilles, beo he amansumod."[27] The prefix would seem to carry the same signification in *Beowulf*
2916–17:

> þær hyne Hetware   hilde genægdon,
> elne geeodon   mid *ofermægene*[28]

and in *Elene* 63–64 we are told that Constantine feared he

26. "Then they saw the host of Pharoah advance from the south, an over-
whelming forest move, the army glitter (the spears were arrayed, the shields
shone, trumpets sang, war approached)."

27. Roger Fowler, "A Late Old English Handbook for the Use of a Con-
fessor," *Anglia* 83 (1965) 23. "If someone by his *overpowering strength* take
a woman or maiden forcibly in fornication against her will, let him be ex-
communicated."

28. "There the Hetware assailed him with war, boldly brought it about
with an overwhelming army."

could never withstand the *mægen unrime* (line 61) of the Huns because he

> hæfde wigena to lyt,
> eaxlgestealna wið *ofermægene* . . .[29]

Occurrences of *ofer-* with the sense "overpowering, over-whelming" are in fact fairly frequent,[30] and if we assume that the prefix carries this meaning in the *oferholt* of *Exodus* 157, the emendation *eoforholt*, the strained meaning "phalanx of shields" (Clark Hall, s.v. *oferholt*), and other desperate measures may be unnecessary.

The overall effect of the "clarifying" variations is to impart to Old English poetry a lucidity and accessibility which distinguishes its style sharply from the more cryptic and mystifying effects of the Old Icelandic poets, who prefer as a rule to designate their referents only once and metaphorically, leaving the reader to puzzle out the meaning as best he can. Something deep in the Anglo-Saxon tradition seems to relish both the metaphorical statement and the clarity which metaphor sometimes lacks, a division of aims illustrated vividly in an Old English glossator's response to a verse of Aldhelm's Anglo-Latin *Ænigma* 95. Speaking of the song which Circe chanted over a pool of water, the flamboyant Aldhelm says, "fontis liquidi maculabat flumina verbis" ("she stained with words the flowing stream of the liquid spring"), which the downright glossator paraphrases, "þæt is, sang on þæt wæter" ("that is, she sang on the water").[31]

At times this impulse toward double statement seems to find reflexes in the narrative art of the Old English poets. The *beamas twegen* of *Exodus* 94 are a cryptic and puzzling allusion until, in a second account thirteen lines later, we are given clarification. At a higher level of narrative structure, we may think of the *Beowulf* poet's representation of Hrethel's grief

29. "He had too few warriors, comrades, against the overwhelming army."

30. See the citations in Joseph Bosworth and T. Northcote Toller, *An Anglo-Saxon Dictionary* (London 1898) s.v. *ofermægen*.

31. Thomas Wright, *Anglo-Saxon and Old English Vocabularies* 1, ed. Richard Wülcker (2nd ed. 2 vols. London 1884) 447.

through an elaborate analogy—that of the hanged man's father and his pathetic lament—which is made clear by the poet's preceding literal statement of the event. Beowulf's report to Hygelac (lines 2000–2151) and the reiterated prophecies of the fall of the Geats offer yet larger-scaled examples of this repetition of identical facts in contrasting terms, while elaborate repetitions in the description of the dragon's hoard (lines 2210–2323) have been shown by Christopher Knipp to be a deliberate and characteristic narrative device.[32] In the past such instances have often been regarded as inadvertencies or lapses of skill. Yet the same mental habit that produced the clarifying variations seems to be at work in these larger structural repetitions, and we might suspect that in all these instances the poets were proceeding by a consistent stylistc principle and were not just aimlessly repeating themselves.

The next and last type of variation to be considered is exemplified by the ensuing list of ten apparently corrupt passages from the Old English poetic corpus. Each passage in the list violates a well-known rule of Old English variation technique: *a poet may not repeat a major word in the two parts of a variation.* If the purpose of variation is to *vary,* to say the same thing in *different* words, then the repetition of a key word contradicts the very motive principle of the figure. Therefore, textual criticism has come to the rescue of these spoiled variations, and in the selection of ten representative examples below I have tried to review some of those rescue missions. I quote the variation as it stands in the unemended manuscript and then indicate to the right the suggested improvements.

1. *Beowulf* 2283–84:

Ða wæs *hord* rasod,	*hlæw*[33]
onboren beaga *hord*	*dæl*[34]

32. Christopher Knipp, "*Beowulf* 2210b–2323: Repetition in the Description of the Dragon's Hoard," *Neuphilologische Mitteilungen* 73 (1972) 775–85.

33. "Then the hoard was rifled, the hoard of rings plundererd." Ferdinand Holthausen, "Beiträge zur Erklärung des altengl. Epos," *Zeitschrift für deutsche Philologie* 37 (1905) 120; Walter J. Sedgefield, *Beowulf* (2nd ed. Manchester 1913).

34. Sophus Bugge, "Zum Beowulf," *Zeitschrift für deutsche Philologie* 4 (1873) 212.

2. *Exodus* 91-92:

þæt þær *drihten* cwom   *dihtan*[35]
weroda *drihten*   *waldend*[36]

3. *Riddle 60*, 12-14:

hu mec seaxes *ord* and seo swiþre hond,
eorles ingeþonc ond *ord* somod,   *ecg,*[37] *oroð*[38]
þingum geþydan

4. *Elene* 214-17:

ond þa his modor het
feran foldwege folca *þreate*
to Iudeum, georne secan
wigena *þreate* hwær se wuldres beam   *werode,*[39] *heape*[40]

5. *Elene* 313-15:

Gangaþ nu snude, snyttro geþencaþ,
weras wisfæste, wordes *cræftige,*   *gleawe*[41]
þa ðe eowre æ æðelum *cræftige*   *gode*[42]

6. *Daniel* 33-34:

þa wearð reðemod rices ðeoden,

---

35. "That the Lord came there, the Lord of hosts." Elliott V. K. Dobbie, review of Edward B. Irving, *The Old English Exodus*, in *Journal of English and Germanic Philology* 53 (1954) 230.

36. "In view of the usual OE principles of variation," Edward B. Irving, *Exodus* (New Haven 1953) 74, is led "to suspect strongly that the original may have had *weroda Waldend.*" But in "New Notes on the Old English Exodus," *Anglia* 90 (1972) 300, Irving defends the manuscript reading, supporting this decision with persuasive parallels from Scripture.

37. "How the point of the knife and that right hand, the man's deep thought and the point together, purposely imprinted me." Georg Herzfeld, *Die Räthsel des Exeterbuches und ihr Verfasser* (Berlin 1890) 69.

38. James M. Hart, "Allotria II," *Modern Language Notes* 17 (1902) 463.

39. "And then he commanded his mother to travel over the earth-way with a band of people to the Jews, to seek with a band of warriors where the tree of glory [was hidden]." Bernhard A. K. ten Brink, "Cynewulfs Elene mit einem glossar herausgegeben von Julius Zupitza," *Anzeiger für deutsches Alterthum* supp. vol. 5 (1879) 59.

40. Ferdinand Holthausen, *Cynewulfs Elene* (Heidelberg and New York 1914).

41. "Go now quickly, think with prudence of men versed in wisdom, skillful of speech, skillful by their nature, who [know] your law." Albert S. Cook, ed., *The Old English Elene, Phoenix, and Physiologus* (New Haven 1919) 13.

42. Holthausen (n. 40 above); cf. Julius Zupitza's note in *Cynewulfs Elene* (Berlin 1899) 14.

unhold *þeoden*   þam þe æhte geaf   *þeodum*[43]
                                              drihten,[44] *þeode*[45]

7. *Daniel* 36-37:
wæron mancynnes   metode *dyrust,*
dugoða *dyrust,*   drihtne leofost   *drymust*[46]
                                                demend[47]
                                                dryhta[48]

8. *Daniel* 321-22:
                oððe *brimfaroþes,*   *brimflodes*[49]
sæfaroða sand   *sæwaroða*[50]

9. *Durham* 7-8:
wuniad in ðem wycum   wilda *deor* monige,
in deope dalum   *deora* ungerim[51]

10. *Charm* 9, 14-15:
Binnan þrym nihtum   cunne ic his *mihta,*
his mægen and his *mihta*   and his mundcræftas   Delete
                                                    and his
                                                   mihta[52]

43. "Then the prince of the realm, the hostile prince, became angry with those to whom he had given dominion." George P. Krapp, *The Anglo-Saxon Poetic Records* 1 (New York 1931) 112; Wilhelm Schmidt, *Die altenglische Dichtung 'Daniel'* (Halle 1907); Ernst A. Kock, "Jubilee Jaunts and Jottings: 250 Contributions to the Interpretation and Prosody of Old West Teutonic Alliterative Poetry," *Lunds Universitets Årsskrift,* new ser. sect. 1 vol. 14 no. 26, page 12.

44. Peter J. Cosijn, "Anglosaxonica II," *Beiträge zur Geschichte der deutschen Sprache und Literatur* 20 (1895) 107.

45. Karl W. Bouterwek, *Caedmon's des Angelsachsen biblische Dichtungen* (Gütersloh 1854) 324. Cf. Thorpe's reading *þeodne* in his edition of the Junius MS.

46. "They were to God the dearest of mankind, the dearest of peoples, most cherished by the Lord." Christian W. M. Grein, *Bibliothek der angelsächsischen Poesie* 2, ed. Richard P. Wülcker (3 vols. Leipzig 1881-98) 478.

47. Cosijn (n. 44 above) 107.

48. Kock (n. 43 above).

49. "Or the sand of the ocean shore, of the shores of the sea." Hertha Marquardt, *Die altenglischen Kenningar* (Halle 1938) 175. (The manuscript reads *brimfaroþæs.*)

50. Christian W. M. Grein, "Zur Textkritik der angelsächsischen Dichter," *Germania* 10 (1865) 416-29 at 419; Grein, *Bibliothek* (n. 46 above) 492; Schmidt (n. 43 above).

51. "Many wild beasts dwell in those places in the deep dales, beasts beyond number."

52. "Within three days I shall know his might, his might and his main,

It should be noticed that the passages requiring emendation appear in a variety of Old English poetic genres and that more than one passage of this type can be found in the same poem. Two of the examples from *Daniel* occur within the scope of only five verses. It should also be noticed that the verbal repetitions which editors have removed never involve any breakdown in meaning, meter, or grammar. The emender's knife has in each instance been wielded solely in the name of a presumptive rule of variation technique. Only the *Durham* passage has been allowed to stand, presumably because there are two independent witnesses to this reading in *Durham*,[53] and scholars were hesitant to assume the same corruption in both lines of transmission. Perhaps editors consoled themselves with the hypothesis that since this is a very late Old English poem, the strength of the prior tradition must have been failing. Such a poet might well have forgotten the classical principle that repetition within variation is impermissible in Old English verse.

But another thought must also suggest itself to the reader who studies this list of putative blunders: the well-known principle of the impermissibility of repetition within variation has been upheld only by virtue of some rather extraordinary exertions on the part of editors and textual scholars. Is it not perhaps possible that these and other passages in which such repetition occurs[54] are perfectly sound as they stand and that there is no rule forbidding repetition within variation?

In considering this question one should also notice that

---

and the powers of his hand." Felix Grendon, "The Anglo-Saxon Charms," *Journal of American Folklore* 22 (1909) 105–237; Godfrid Storms, *Anglo-Saxon Magic* (The Hague 1948) 210.

53. The repeated *deor . . . deora* appears in both University Library, Cambridge, MS Ff.i.27 and in the version which George Hickes printed in his *Linguarum vett. septentrionalium thesaurus grammatico-criticus et archaeologicus* 1 (3 vols. Oxford 1705) 178–79, from the now lost Cotton MS Vitellius D.xx.

54. I have noted four further passages with such repetition in *Beowulf*, two in *Maldon*, and a sprinkling of occurrences in the elegies, the gnomic poetry, the *Paris Psalter* (where the parallelism and repetitions of the Vulgate no doubt reinforced the tendency), and in *Instructions for Christians*.

repetition within variations would hardly be an isolated phenomenon in Old English verse. An examination of any fairly extensive section of the corpus will reveal verbal repetition within coordinate series linked by conjunctions, repetition of the same word or morpheme to establish the alliterative stave of a long-line (although these, like repetitions within variations, will often be removed by editorial emendation), repetition within a single sentence or within contiguous sentences, paronomastic repetition of the kind that Roberta Frank explores,[55] and ornamental polyptota such as *æðele be æðelum, werige mid werigum, wundor æfter wundre, stan from stane, halig haligne, cyninga cyning, of dæge on dæge,* and *in woruld worulda,* all of which occur within the single poem *Andreas.* As an example of how the presence of other types of repetition might suggest that repetition within variations was not as abhorrent to the Anglo-Saxon ear as we have long assumed, we may examine once again the tenth passage in the above list. Preceding this passage in the ninth charm are the following verses (lines 7–9):

> find þæt feoh   and fere þæt feoh
> and hafa þæt feoh   and heald þæt feoh
> and fere ham þæt feoh[56]

Immediately following the variation containing repetition, moreover, is this line:

> Eall he *weornige,*   swa syre wudu *weornie*[57]

That successive scholars should pause amid this din of incantatory repetition in order to excise a single repetition from a variation bears impressive witness to the strength of our belief in the conjectural rule that variation can never involve repetition.

That rule, I believe, is an invention of modern scholars, not of the scopas. Repetition within variation, like repetition

puns

55. Roberta Frank, "Some Uses of Paronomasia in Old English Scriptual Verse," *Speculum* 47 (1972) 207–26.
56. "Find that herd, and convey that herd, and keep that herd and hold that herd, and bring that herd home."
57. "May he all wither, as dry wood may wither."

within other, similarly close syntactical structures, would appear to have been a consciously cultivated stylistic device, and the manuscript reading in each of the passages cited above should be allowed to stand without further challenge. We should try, moreover, to sense the special effect the poet is intending when he adopts such repetitions in his variations. Sometimes the repetition seems to throw emphasis on the word repeated, as in the third example, in which *ord* appears twice. At other times, paradoxically, the repetition of a noun seems to give greater emphasis to a modifier which occurs with but one of the occurrences of the repeated word. In the second example above, for instance, the iteration of *drihten* seems somehow to lay stress on *weroda*, the effect being to emphasize God's role as Lord of *hosts*. If the second *drihten* is changed to *Waldend*, as Edward B. Irving originally suggested in his edition, the contrastive force of the variation would be dissipated among the two different elements of the variation rather than focused on the one differing element *weroda*. Other repetitive variations in the list may well have been intended for yet other effects.

There is in Old English poetry such pervasive use of artful synonymy, of contrastive restatement in different words, that we sometimes overlook just how extensive and various are the stylistic uses of exact verbal repetition. But repetition is used, and in many different ways. An obvious example is those rhetorical units which Adeline C. Bartlett has called "envelope patterns."[58] Here the repetition of words or groups of words at the beginning and at the close of self-contained segments of narrative effectively and functionally mark these sections off from the surrounding text. Another use of repetition within similar compass is in those fugal patterns of recurrence which

58. Adeline C. Bartlett, *The Larger Rhetorical Patterns in Anglo-Saxon Poetry* (New York 1935) 9. A special case is the repeated epithet *ece dryhten* in Caedmon's *Hymn*, a repetition which John C. Pope, *Seven Old English Poems* (Indianapolis 1966) 52, sees as a kind of burden marking off the poem into stanza-like units. Another special case is the *dúnadh* pattern (as in "The Capture of the Five Boroughs") discussed by Patrick L. Henry, "A Celtic-English Prosodic Figure," *Zeitschrift für Celtische Philologie* 29 (1962) 91–99.

John O. Beaty long ago called "echo-words" and which James L. Rosier has more recently characterized as "generative composition."[59] These uses of repetition produce a verbal intertexture which contributes more than we consciously realize, I suspect, to the unity of style and harmony of phrase that we all sense in the best Old English poetry.

A more specifically pointed use of repetition may be seen in the Unferth intermezzo of *Beowulf*, where the hero's repetition of Unferth's own words in his reply to the hostile *þyle* gives force and sting to the rejoinder. Here repetition functions dramatically within the narrative action itself. But the poet also uses repetition as a way of making implicit comments on his narrative, as when he embellishes the description of Beowulf's funeral rites at the end of the poem with echoes and epithets from the Scyld funeral which introduced the narrative. Being convinced, as I am, that the formulaic quality of Old English poetry did not deaden the ear to nuances, I sense stylistic effect and poetic meaning in these echoes. A similar effect and meaning result, I believe, from the way Beowulf, in his old age, falls heir to the epithets which had earlier described Hrothgar—*eald eþelweard, folces hyrde, gumcystum god, har hilderinc, frod cyning, rices hyrde*, and so on—while Wiglaf inherits the epithets for the youthful Beowulf, such as *hæle hildedeor* and *feþecempa*.[60] The pathos of aging and the mystery of the hero's inevitable departure from this life

59. John O. Beaty, "The Echo-Word in *Beowulf* with a Note on the *Finnsburg Fragment*," *PMLA* 49 (1934) 365-73; James L. Rosier, "Generative Composition in *Beowulf*," *English Studies* 58 (1977) 193-203. The phenomenon is also explored by Eugene R. Kintgen, "Echoic Repetition in Old English Poetry, Especially *The Dream of the Rood*," *Neuphilologische Mitteilungen* 75 (1974) 202-23, who argues that such repetitions are conscious artistic effects which function as both stylistic and structural devices in the poem. His argument would seem to gain strength from the demonstration by a later scholar that Old English poets were capable of eschewing such repetition when they found it artistically preferable to do so; see Geoffrey R. Russom's "Artful Avoidance of the Useful Phrase in *Beowulf, The Battle of Maldon* and *Fates of the Apostles*," which is to appear in *Studies in Philology*.

60. See William Whallon, "Formulas for Heroes in the 'Iliad' and in 'Beowulf,'" *Modern Philology* 63 (1965) 102.

acquire deeper poignancy through these verbal echoes that
emphasize the rhythmic recurrence of such events in the
heroic past. Verbal repetition plays a part, it would seem, in
some of the poem's best moments, and if this is true of the
larger structure of *Beowulf*, we should perhaps be all the
readier to accept repetition in the smaller structures, such as
variation.[61]

In isolating for analysis two of the many types of variation in
Old English poetry, I have tried to illustrate more than one
way in which we can profit from study of this kind. This scrutiny may lead to a finer discernment of the local effects which a
poet sought with a certain kind of variation if we examine
these variations in aggregate. Indeed, by examining them
together, we can at times even throw light on the textual interpretation of a difficult passage. Taking a broader view, we can
perceive analogies between the poet's strategies in his use of
variation and his procedures at other levels of diction, and on
occasion, in the larger narrative structures.[62] Such analogies
should not be pressed too far, but they can be a helpful guide
to understanding the stylistic intentions in a body of poetry for
which we have no *ars poetica* and no *Skáldskaparmál*.

61. Nor should we look askance on emendations which introduce repetition into variations if other considerations warrant the change. See, for
example, the meritorious emendation of *adloman* to *aðlogan* (with the atten-
dant repetition of *-logan* in *wærlogan* and *aðlogan*) in *Guthlac* 912 proposed
by Herbert D. Meritt, *Fact and Lore about Old English Words* (Stanford
1954) 5–6.

62. In arguing this point my method has been the reverse of Joan Blom-
field's, who, in "The Style and Structure of *Beowulf*," *Review of English
Studies* 14 (1938) 396–403, tried to demonstrate how "analysis of style is . . .
a justifiable approach to analysis of structure" (p. 397).

ACTION IN *BEOWULF* AND OUR
PERCEPTION OF IT

Peter Clemoes

I WANT TO BEGIN at the "perception" end of my subject. And I want first to point out that Old English poetic narrative does not have what I would call "audience perspective": in other words, description is not directed toward the viewpoint, outside the scene, which we as hearers or readers of a poem might be supposed to have. This kind of outward organization is, of course, common in later literature. A passage from a fourteenth-century poem, still in the alliterative tradition, *Sir Gawain and the Green Knight*, will serve as an example. When Gawain, led by a guide, is close to the Green Chapel, he makes his last, critical choice. The guide is about to depart, his job done. But, before going, he stops and makes the knight a tempting offer: "Keep away from the place and avoid certain death," he advises. "If you do, I swear I will never let on!" "No, I have to see this through," says Gawain (or words to that effect), and sets spurs to his horse. This moment of decision comes after the knight and his companion had followed a tortuous track through woods

> Til hit watz sone sesoun þat þe sunne ryses
> > þat tyde.
> Þay were on a hille ful hyȝe,
> Þe quyte snaw lay bisyde;
> Þe burne þat rod hym by
> Bede his mayster abide. (2085-90)

The poet has placed the two men, freshly emerged from a

dense wood, on a snowcovered hilltop at sunrise. To our mind's eye they are silhouetted there when Gawain experiences his moment of truth. We apprehend him at the center of a sharply focused image. We see the two men in their setting as they cannot see themselves.

By contrast take the scene of Beowulf's embarkation for his *wilsið* to Denmark:

> flota wæs on ýðum,
> bat under beorge.[1]   (210b-11a)

A ship was on the waves under a cliff. Beowulf has ordered a boat (*ýðlida*, a "wave traveller" [198b]) to be prepared and has been leading his picked men towards the shore; and then this boat materializes, so to speak:

> Fyrst forð gewat;   flota wæs on ýðum,
> bat under beorge.[2]

But what is our point of view (or points of view)? Are we on the shore beside the boat? Are we on the clifftop? No, we are not thought of as anywhere in particular. There is no feature in this description which specifically directs it towards us. We are left to look after ourselves. The relationships are internal to the scene: the ship fulfills Beowulf's intention; it is on the waves as a "floater" because of those waves; the interaction of boat and sea is what matters. But if we are not localized, neither is our view in any way restricted. There is no conditioned limitation in our apprehension. The statements come to us as absolutes.

The medium of such statements in Old English poetry is language concerned with synthesis, with what is general in the particular.[3] The wholeness of perception resides in terms which, though responsive to the associations of context, are usable in many poems. It works through (mostly) unparticularized expressions of analogy ("seahorse" for "ship") or connection ("ring-hall"). It goes *pari passu* with a rhetoric of universals—in *Beowulf*, Grendel's descent from Cain, com-

---

1. My quotations are from *Beowulf and the Fight at Finnsburg*, ed. Friedrich Klaeber (3rd ed. Boston 1936).

2. "Time passed; the floater was on the waves, the boat under the cliff."

3. See Calder's essay above in this volume, passim.

parison of Beowulf with other heroes, inclusive generalizations, and relating human attributes and actions to *wyrd* and God. It carries an implication of omniscience which some mistakenly systematize intellectually as allegory. And, incidentally, it makes most Old English poems difficult to date: a poem is not intimately responsive to the occasion of its origin but stands at a distance from it, so that an "historical" author or "historical" audience can be discerned, if at all, only through accidentals and not essentials.

In *Beowulf* the narrator mediates between events and us. He does not address us directly in the manner of

> Herken, lordyngys þat ben trewe,
> And y wol ȝou telle of Syr Orphewe.

Addressing an Old English audience as "you" belongs to the homilist—for special effect, according to the rules of rhetoric. For instance, in "De Fide Catholica,"[4] his homily on the apostles' creed, Wulfstan uses this form of address only to introduce each of the three main stages in his treatment of the creed and refers to himself as "I" in relation to this "you" only at the last of these stages.[5] The nearest an Old English poet comes to this is when using the inclusive *we*—in exhortation, for example:

> Uton we hycgan   hwær we ham agen,
> ond þonne geþencan   hu we þider cumen.[6]

> (*The Seafarer* 117-18)

4. *The Homilies of Wulfstan*, ed. Dorothy Bethurum (Oxford 1957) no. 7, pp. 157-65.

5. His introduction begins "Leofan men, doð swa eow mycel þearf is, understandað þæt ælc cristen man ah micle þearfe þæt he his cristendomes gescead wite, 7 þæt he cunne rihtne geleafan rihtlice understandan" (3-6); his central exposition of the creed begins "Leofan menn, understandað swyðe georne þæt ge æfre habban rihtne geleafan on ænne ælmihtigne God" (26-27); and his conclusion begins "Nu ic hæbbe eow areht rihtne geleafan" (159). ("Dear people, do as there is great need for you to do, understand that each Christian has great need to comprehend his Christianity, and to be able to understand true belief truly"; "Dear people, understand very carefully, so that you always have true belief in one almighty God"; and "Now I have explained to you true belief.")

6. "Let us think where we have our home, and then consider how we may reach it."

The *Beowulf* narrator's relationship with us is more impersonal and distant. Stanley Greenfield has aptly termed him a
"voice."[7] This voice selects what we know—giving us at times
significant information not shared by a protagonist—and (to
use Greenfield's words) "validates the way or ways in which it
understands and wishes its audience to understand" events.[8]
But it remains the voice of traditional corporate wisdom,
indistinguishable from the kind the protagonists utter themselves—"þæt wæs god cyning!" (11b etc.) and the like—and
claims only to share in collective indirect knowledge:

> Hwæt, we Gardena   in geardagum
> þeodcyninga   þrym gefrunon.[9] (1–2)

In other Old English poems a narrator may assert that he is
relating what he has experienced for himself:

> Mæg ic be me sylfum   soðgied wrecan.[10]
>
> *(The Seafarer* 1)

How subtle and profound, as well as dramatic, an impression
this can make we know well from first the dreamer and then
the Cross in *The Dream of the Rood.* But no Old English narrator ever explicitly invites us, the audience, in our imagination to see and hear happenings for ourselves, to be on the spot
and have our own spectators' relationship to events. Only in
later literature could a chorus speak like this:

> Suppose that you have seen
> The well-appointed king at Hampton pier
> Embark his royalty; and his brave fleet
> With silken streamers the young Phoebus fanning:
> Play with your fancies, and in them behold
> Upon the hempen tackle ship-boys climbing;
> Hear the shrill whistle which doth order give
> To sounds confused: behold the threaden sails,

7. Stanley B. Greenfield, "The Authenticating Voice in *Beowulf*," *Anglo-
Saxon England* 5 (1976) 51–62, esp. 53.

8. Ibid.

9. "Lo, we have heard of the glory of the Gar-Danes, kings of the people,
in days long ago."

10. "I can tell a true story about myself."

Borne with the invisible and creeping wind,
Draw the huge bottoms through the furrow'd sea,
Breasting the lofty surge: O, do but think
You stand upon the rivage and behold
A city on the inconstant billows dancing;
For so appears this fleet majestical,
Holding due course to Harfleur.

(Shakespeare, *Henry V*, III, Prologue 3-17)

Evidently Beowulf's embarkation for Denmark is simply not thought to be accessible to our imagination in that particular way. He and his men go on board, stow their equipment in the hold and push off out to sea. Action and description interlace. First comes the setting of the scene, already quoted,

> flota wæs on yðum,
> bat under beorge;

then comes the boarding,

> beornas gearwe
> on stefn stigon;[11]

then the movement of the sea against the shore,

> streamas wundon,
> sund wið sande;[12]

then the stowing of equipment,

> secgas bæron
> on bearm nacan   beorhte frætwe,
> guðsearo geatolic;[13]

then the pushing off,

> guman ut scufon,
> weras on wilsið   wudu bundenne;[14]

11. "Men, ready, mounted the prow."
12. "Currents flowed, the sea against the sand."
13. "Men carried shining equipment, splendid armor, into the bosom of the ship."
14. "Men, warriors, pushed out the joined wood on the wished-for journey."

and then the movement of the boat out to sea,

> gewat þa ofer wægholm   winde gefysed
> flota famiheals   fugle gelicost.[15]

The actions are as unqualified as is their setting: *on stefn stigon, bæron on bearm nacan, ut scufon*. The particularization lies elsewhere: the men are *gearwe*; the equipment which they stow on board is *beorhte frætwe, guðsearo geatolic*. Above all, the boat on which they embark is part of a changing set of relationships. At first it is associated with both sea and shore—on the waves and under a cliff; then, while the boat is being boarded and loaded, the sea is brought into its own direct connection with the shore,

> streamas wundon,
> sund wið sande;

finally, with the pushing off, we hear no more of the shore, and the boat, the sea and the wind are brought together. In our apprehension, the boat progresses from a stationary, definite location to an indefinitely localized movement in counterpoint to the action of the moving element (the sea) against the static element (the shore). That this interaction is organic is borne out by the vocabulary: the sea is at first waves, then currents with depth, and finally a *wægholm*, a whole sea of waves; the boat changes from a utilitarian thing of specific parts, a prow and a hold, to a whole object designed to withstand the sea, *wudu bundenne*, and finally becomes a thing of pure movement, a foamy-necked floater like a bird. Both boat and sea undergo development within their distinctive beings. They seem akin in so doing. The embarkation is presented as a process of nature. We sense the fundamental character of this *wilsið*. The poet's art lies in giving us a strong sense of the boat's essential change without impeding it with any overlay of external description.

This view of the inner principles of things is like Aldhelm's in the concluding enigma of his collection. (I am not, let me

15. "Then the foamy-necked floater, driven by the wind, went over the sea of waves like a bird."

hasten to say, about to mount an argument that Aldhelm had anything to do with the composition of *Beowulf*: I wish only to point to a general similarity of conception.) The nature which Aldhelm expounds in this riddle comprises all the tendencies possessed by the individual parts of nature, a comprehensive potentiality to be most vividly appreciated from manifestations in extreme contrast:

> Frigidior brumis necnon candente pruina,
> Cum sim Vulcani flammis torrentibus ardens,
> Dulcior in palato quam lenti nectaris haustus
> Dirior et rursus quam glauca absinthia campi.
> Mando dapes mordax lurconum more Ciclopum,
> Cum possim iugiter sine victu vivere felix.
> Plus pernix aquilis, Zephiri velocior alis,
> Necnon accipitre properantior, et tamen horrens
> Lumbricus et limax et tarda testudo palustris
> Atque, fimi soboles sordentis, cantarus ater
> Me dicto citius vincunt certamine cursus.[16] (C, 29-39)

A species—the eagle, the hawk, the earthworm, the snail or whatever—is distinctive according to the particular part of nature's vast potential it reveals. Indeed the very fascination of the riddle genre itself is to recognize what a creature is from what it manifests. Or again, it is a nature of strong innate forces—this time forever locked in divinely controlled conflict

16.　　"Colder am I than winter and hoar frost,
　　　　Although I glow with Vulcan's flaming heat;
　　　　Sweeter than slow-dripped nectar to the taste,
　　　　More bitter than grey wormwood of the field;
　　　　Like gluttonous Cyclopes I gulp down food,
　　　　Though foodless I could always happy live.
　　　　Swifter than eagles or than Zephyr's wings,
　　　　And fleeter than the hawk am I, and yet
　　　　The cowering earthworm, snail, and tortoise slow,
　　　　Haunter of fens, and the black worm that springs
　　　　From ordure foul, faster than tongue can tell
　　　　Each could surpass me should we run a race."

The Riddles of Aldhelm, ed. and trans. James Hall Pitman, Yale Studies in English 67 (New Haven 1925; repr. Hamden Conn. 1970) 62-65.

—which King Alfred depicts in his version of Boethius's *De Consolatione Philosophiae*:

Swa hæfð se ælmihtiga God geheaðorade ealle his gescefta mid his anwealde þæt heora ælc winð wið oðer, 7 þeah wræðeð oðer, þ hie ne moton toslupan, ac bioð gehwerfde eft to þam ilcan ryne þe hie ær urnon, 7 swa weorðað eft geedniwade. Swa hi hit fagiað þ þa wiðerweardan gesceafta ægðer ge hie betwux him winnað, ge eac fæste sibbe betwux him healdað. Swa nu fyr deð, 7 wæter 7 lyft 7 eorðe, 7 manega oðra gesceafta þe beoð a swa ungeðwæra betwux him swa swa hi beoð; 7 þeah hi beoð swa geþwæra þætte no þ an þæt hi magon geferan beon, ac þy furðor þ heora furðum nan buton oðrum beon ne mæg. Ac a sceal þ wiðerwearde þ oðer wiðerwearde gemetgian.[17]

(Let me once more disavow any intention of claiming a direct link!) Ælfric, late in the Anglo-Saxon period, similarly thinks that all natural objects contain inner elements which reveal their presence when given occasion:

Nis nan lichamlic ðing þe næbbe ða feower gesceafta him mid. þæt is lyft. 7 fyr. eorðe. 7 wæter; On ælcum lichaman sind þas feower ðing. nimm ænne sticcan. 7 gnid to sumum ðince. hit hatað þærrihte of ðam fyre þe him on lutað; Forbærn ðone oðerne ende. þonne gæð se wæta ut æt ðam oðrum ende mid ðam smice;[18]

17. *King Alfred's Old English Version of Boethius De Consolatione Philosophiae*, ed. Walter John Sedgefield (Oxford 1899) 49, lines 5-16. ("The almighty God has so restrained all his creatures with his power that each of them contends with the other and yet supports the other, so that they may not slacken but are returned to the same course that they have run before and are thus renewed. They are at variance so that the opposed creatures both conflict with one another and maintain firm peace between themselves. Thus do fire and water and air and earth, and many other creatures which are every bit as contentious among themselves as they are, and yet are so in agreement that they not only can be companions but also cannot even exist without one another. The one contrary must control the other contrary all the time.") I have corrected MS *sæ* to *lyft*.

18. *Ælfric's De Temporibus Anni* 10.9-11, ed. Heinrich Henel, Early English Text Society o.s. 213 (1942) 74. ("There is no bodily thing which does not have with it the four creatures air, fire, earth and water. These four things are in every body. Take a stick and rub it against something. It immediately grows hot from the fire which is hidden in it. Burn the one end and the water goes out at the other with the smoke.")

And I think Anglo-Saxon art shows insight into inner forces. The decorator, who, during the first half of the tenth century, drew and painted remarkable ornamental initials in the Oxford, Bodleian, Tanner 10 manuscript of the Old English Bede, expresses a power of gymnastic movement in his human figures without portraying an anatomy which is externally realistic. What is important to him is that his creatures— human beings and full-bodied beasts—in their vigor hold one another in check in the shapes of the letters. The *Beowulf* poet is not composing a riddle or a treatise on philosophy or on natural science or decorating a manuscript, but he shows the same sense of the innate forces of nature when he says that the men returning in high spirits after following the dying Grendel's tracks to the blood-stained mere

> hleapan leton,
> on geflit faran   fealwe mearas.[19] (864b-65)

The men allowed their steeds to exert their natural tendency, identified as a certain kind of movement (*hleapan*) and as movement in competition (*on geflit faran*). It would be quite foreign to the poet's mentality to give the act of galloping any further description. Movement for him is not a matter for objective examination and analysis, as it was to become in the Renaissance. His descriptive adverbs, for instance, make this plain. They are rare and when they occur—*earfoðlice* (1636), *ellenlice* (2122), *fæste* (760), *georne* (2294), *hrædlice* (963), *hraþe* (224), *snude* (2568), *unmurnlice* (449), *unwearnum* (741), *yrringa* (1565)—have to do primarily with the doer's attitude to the action, his involvement in it, not with the impression which the action makes outside as a movement: somebody is doing something bravely, or eagerly, or ruthlessly, or angrily, and so on. Movement in *Beowulf* is not portrayed as a detachable outward concept: it merely identifies action as part of the doer; action belongs to him as an innate, inherent attribute—it is what philosophers call "immanent."

It is an essential attribute. The hallmark of a *mære þeoden* is that he distributes treasure (*Beowulf* 2381b-84a). To

19. "let their bay horses gallop, compete."

deprive a *nicor*, a "water-monster," of *yðgewinn*, "wave-strife," is to kill it (*Beowulf* 1432b–34a). If you refer to an animal as a *hæðstapa*—a hart in *Beowulf* (1368a), a wolf in *The Fortunes of Men* (13a)—you are classifying it according to the environment it moves in. If you compare a ship driven by the wind to a bird (*Beowulf* 217–18), you are likening it to the creature that pre-eminently possesses that kind of movement. Beings such as Grendel and the dragon are such powerful narrative images because action is fundamentally indivisible from actor. To the Anglo-Saxons innate menacing action was *draconitas* and the like. These beasts constitute the idea. That is their reality. That is why they are in the poem *Beowulf* and in the initials of the Tanner manuscript.

This way of thinking about action creates certain ways of expression. Preference for active rather than passive verbs emphasizes the connection between actions and their agents: the *Beowulf* poet's way of saying "he was gripped by . . ." is

> . . . hine se modega   mæg Hygelaces
> hæfde be honda.[20]   (813–14a)

Priority of nouns and adjectives over finite verbs works to the same effect: *æfter leodhryre*, "after prince-fall" (2030a), twins actor and action as "after a prince has fallen" does not. This is even more evident if the equivalent finite verb would be passive; compare *æfter mundgripe*, "after hand-grip" (1938a), with "after he had been seized." Nouns such as these are not truly abstract; the *grap*, "grasp," which Grendel was deprived of, like the *grap* which deprived him of it—*wiste his fingra geweald / on grames grapum*, "he knew the control of his fingers was in the grasp of an angry man" (764b–65a)—combines potential, location and action all rolled into one:

>   Þæt wæs tacen sweotol,
> syþðan hildedeor   hond alegde,
> earm ond eaxle   —þær wæs eal geador
> Grendles grape—   under geapne hrof.[21] (833b–36)

20. "Him the brave kinsman of Hygelac had by the hand."
21. "That was a clear sign, after the man brave in battle laid down the hand, arm and shoulder—there all together was Grendel's grasp—under the spacious roof."

Grap is the active principle of the conflict:[22] the fight consists
of one person's *grap* against another's. Then, of course, there
is the agent noun to make the agent-action relationship explicit, as in *swa he bena wæs*, "as he had been asker" (3140b),
and *þeah ðu þinum broðrum to banan wurde*, "though you
have been your brothers' killer" (587). Compound agent
nouns are a much used means of description. For instance,
Grendel coming to Heorot and there meeting defeat at
Beowulf's hands, is characterized successively as <u>*sceadugenga*,</u>
"shadow-walker" (703a), *scynscaþa*,[23] "phantom-injurer"
(707a), *manscaða*, "crime-injurer" (712a and 737b), *hearm-
scaþa*, "harm-injurer" (766a), *synscaða*, "sin-injurer" (801b),
and *cwealmcuma*, "slaughter-comer" (792a).

Connectives refer to the inner nature of action. For
instance, *oþþæt* links two actions "internally," without "external" discrimination, in the account of Beowulf's voyage to
Denmark after the embarkation:

> Gewat þa ofer wægholm   winde gefysed
> flota famiheals   fugle gelicost,
> oð þæt ymb antid   oþres dogores
> wundenstefna   gewaden hæfde,
> þæt ða liðende   land gesawon,
> brimclifu blican,   beorgas steape,
> side sænæssas.[24] (217–23a)

The two actions are the movement of the boat on the sea and
the men's perception of land.[25] This journey is not a travelling
through space objectively conceived, "between two points on a
Mercator Projection" (as Loren C. Gruber has recently put it

22. As such, it is central to Beowulf's boasts beforehand (438b–39a and
635b–36a).

23. Klaeber's emendation (MS *synscaþa*).

24. "Then the foamy-necked floater, driven by the wind, went over the
sea of waves like a bird, until after due time of another day the curved prow
had journeyed, so that the seafarers saw land, seacliffs shining, steep hills,
broad headlands."

25. Cf. J. W. Richard Lindemann, *Old English Preverbal "Ge-": Its
Meaning* (Charlottesville Va. 1970) 39 and 60, on verbs of sense perception
as verbs of motion.

in a perceptive study[26]), but, as Gruber realizes, it is a quali-
tative development by which the uncomplicated action of the
ship is replaced by, issues in, makes directly possible, another,
fuller, more significant action by the men. Characteristically
connectives of this kind bind together the announcement of
Beowulf's death to his people (2900-3027). The message is
that revenge by the Franks and the Swedes for past killings,[27]
funerary burning of the treasure paid for with Beowulf's life,
and desolation lie ahead. The thought moves to and fro
between specific actions and states of mind, pregnant with
counter-action, by means of temporal adverbs and conjunctions. This is easiest to illustrate from the sequence to do with
the Franks. First an affecting picture of Beowulf lying dead,
with the dragon, which has killed him, lifeless beside him and
with Wiglaf, exhausted, sitting by them both, actualizes the
present: it begins "Nu is . . . ." Then in this present is placed
expectation of war after the Franks have heard of Beowulf's
death: "Nu ys . . . syððan . . . ." The Franks' attitude of mind
was created after Hygelac raided the Rhineland and was killed
there: "Wæs . . . syððan . . . ." It has persisted ever since:
". . . wæs a syððan . . . ." An action of Hygelac has passed into
wroht, "offence," which, now that Beowulf has been killed,
will pass into *orleghwil*, "a time of war," with the inevitability
of time itself. And so it is throughout the parallel sequence to
do with the Geats' killing of the Swedish Ongentheow—rich in
psychological understanding of an act which inevitably created
resentment in the one people (the Swedes) and gratitude in the
other (the Geats)—and throughout the return to the present
and the uncompromising forward look to Beowulf's funeral
pyre, these topics involving no less than twenty-five temporal
adverbs and conjunctions. But, when this retrogressive temporal chain of the deaths of kings—Beowulf's, Hygelac's,
Ongentheow's—is joined to a final desolate image of the
future, the link changes:

26. Loren C. Gruber, "Motion, Perception, and *ofþæt* in *Beowulf*," *In
Geardagum*, ed. Loren C. Gruber and Dean Loganbill (Denver 1974) 31-37
at 33.

27. Only general knowledge of the past is shown in the case of the Franks
but close knowledge of the details of a campaign in the other.

> Forðon sceall gar wesan
> monig morgenceald   mundum bewunden,
> hafen on handa,   nalles hearpan sweg
> wigend weccean,   ac se wonna hrefn
> fus ofer fægum   fela reordian,
> earne secgan,   hu him æt æte speow,
> þenden he wið wulf   wæl reafode.[28] (3021b-27)

Forðon connects vitally different kinds of action. Hitherto doers have relentlessly done and been done by; henceforth human beings are the mere instruments and victims of action. This deprivation of their birthright, consequential upon what has been done before, strikes a chill into our hearts. Language is indeed used in this poem to make statements about the fundamentals of action within space and time.

The sense that action belongs to someone has implications for story-telling. For one thing action itself can become submerged in a way that may offend us moderns. Explanation, comment and digression of all kinds crowd in. When the dragon is at last dealt a fatal blow, the action is made subordinate to the implications which the blow has for the man who delivers it:

> . . . sio hand gebarn
> modiges mannes,   þær he his mæges healp,
> þæt he þone niðgæst   nioðor hwene sloh.[29] (2697b-99)

Not uncommonly the outcome of an action takes precedence, as when Beowulf effects a crucial recovery at a desperate stage of his fight with Grendel's mother:

> witig Drihten,
> rodera Rædend   hit on ryht gesced
> yðelice,   syþðan he eft astod.[30] (1554b-56)

28. "Therefore shall many a spear, cold in the morning, be grasped by hand, raised in the hand; not at all shall the sound of the harp rouse warriors, but the dark raven eager for the doomed shall speak much, tell the eagle how he ate well while he plundered the dead with the wolf."

29. ". . . the hand of the brave man burned, as he helped his kinsman, so that he struck the enemy somewhat lower down."

30. "The wise Lord, Ruler of the skies, easily decided it rightly after he stood up again."

Evidently the poet is not intent on using a sequence of action
for suspense leading to resolution in a contrived climax. He is
not as concerned as a modern author might be to exploit action
for its own sake as an exciting narrative element. But compelling narrative is brought about when two protagonists are in
conflict; the confrontation of *grap* and *grap* in Beowulf's fight
with Grendel is total:

> ræhte ongean
> feond mid folme;   he onfeng hraþe
> inwitþancum.[31]   (747b–49a)

> wæs gehwæþer oðrum
> lifigende lað.[32]   (814b–15a)

The opposing attitudes of mind, the one (Beowulf's) remaining firm, the other (Grendel's) changing suddenly from exultation to fear, criss-cross dramatically.

Identity of actor and action has important consequences for
characterization. Beowulf's lack of fear when he is about to set
out for his critical fight with the dragon is accounted for, not
merely by a general reference to the many dangers which he
has survived since his victories over Grendel and Grendel's
mother (2349b–54a), but also by recounting the positive actions he took to surmount two of the greatest of these dangers
(2354b–96), because such past actions characterize him irrevo-
cably. They are part of the man. What has been done is part of
the doer, whether that is a man or a sword, accumulating—
like a man's wisdom (indeed active experience is an essential
part of that wisdom)—as the doer's existence proceeds. The
poet's predominant interest is how a person's actions successively characterize him and how these actions relate to the
forces within him, to the forces that act through or on him,
and to the forces that he acts on. *Mægen* is to be understood as
an innate force (not mere tautology) when Beowulf is first
introduced,

> se wæs moncynnes   mægenes strengest
> on þæm dæge   þysses lifes[33]   (196–97),

31. "The enemy reached out against him with his hand; he quickly took
hold of him with hostile intent."

32. "Each while alive was the other's enemy."

33. "He was the strongest of mankind in might on that day of this life."

and when the seal is set on Grendel's inescapable defeat,

> Heold hine fæste
> se þe manna wæs   mægene strengest
> on þæm dæge   þysses lifes.[34] (788b-90)

Elements outside the doer such as *wyrd* are at once potent and poignant—*wyrd* which, as *The Seafarer* has it, *biþ swiþre* . . . *þonne ænges monnes gehygd*, "is stronger . . . than the mind of any man" (115b-16); *wyrd*, not intellectually defined (though much about it can be recognized by analysis), but the felt force which is experienced in events and which no man, only God, can control. In *Beowulf wyrd* is death-bearing. The hero acknowledges this power (*Gæð a wyrd swa hio scel!* "Fate always goes as it must!" [455b]), knows that it can be challenged (*Wyrd oft nereð / unfægne eorl, þonne his ellen deah!* "Fate often protects a man who is not doomed, when his courage is good!" [572b-73]), and finally suffers:

> Him wæs geomor sefa,
> wæfre ond wælfus,   wyrd ungemete neah,
> se ðone gomelan   gretan sceolde,
> secean sawle hord,   sundur gedælan
> lif wið lice.[35]   (2419b-23a)

Within interacting forces a person's actions constitute his identity. They involve moral values, questions to do with the realization of potential. For Hrothgar an all-important difference in applying an endowment of exceptional strength marks Beowulf off from Heremod:

> "Eal þu hit geþyldum healdest,
> mægen mid modes snyttrum,"[36]   (1705b-06a)

he declares to Beowulf,

> "Ne wearð Heremod swa
> eaforum Ecgwelan,   Ar-Scyldingum;

34. "He who was the strongest of men in might on that day of this life held him fast."

35. "His mind was sad, restless and ready for death; fate, which was to approach the old man, seek the treasure of the soul, separate life from the body, was very near indeed."

36. "You keep it all steadily, strength with wisdom of mind."

> ne geweox he him to willan . . .
> ðeah þe hine mihtig God   mægenes wynnum,
> eafeþum stepte,   ofer ealle men
> forð gefremede.   Hwæþere him on ferhþe greow
> breosthord blodreow.''[37]   (1709b-11a, 1716-19a)

A man's "character" is what others think of his actions—his reputation. Personal relationships are born of shared action: Hrothgar gives his love to Beowulf as to a son; the Geats recoil from using any part of the great treasure which has been bought with the life of their brave leader.

Characterization through action makes "set-piece" description of protagonists inappropriate, whereas evaluations of performed action—Hrothgar's "sermon" for instance—are to the point. So too, after action, are responses such as gift-giving or revenge, and the confidence or loyalty or fear of others before or during action: the sorrow, terror and helplessness of the Danes establish Grendel's malignant potency as *ellengæst* in feud with God; the successive reactions of *snotere ceorlas* at home, the Danish coastguard, Wulfgar the *ar ond ombiht*, Hrothgar himself, Unferth and Wealhtheow do likewise for Beowulf in action as hero. Knowledge brought to bear by the narrator is important: he alone refers to Grendel's descent from Cain. (The Danes do not even know whether he has had a father.) "Character" as reputation requires comparison: the *guma . . . gidda gemindig*, the "man . . . mindful of songs" (868), sets the scale for Beowulf's *mærðo*, "renown" (857a), after his defeat of Grendel, by singing of the glorious Sigemund and the notorious Heremod.

More organically still, the primacy of the actor-action relationship makes the narrative "psychological" and the poet's technique is directed to bringing out this "psychological" quality. Beowulf and his men sight the coastline of Denmark:

> oð þæt ymb antid   oþres dogores
> wundenstefna   gewaden hæfde,

37. "Heremod did not become so to the sons of Ecgwela, the Ar-Scyldings; he did not develop as a pleasure to them . . . although mighty God had exalted him in the joys of might, in strength, had advanced him beyond all men. Yet bloodthirsty thoughts grew in his mind."

þæt ða liðende   land gesawon,
brimclifu blican,   beorgas steape,
side sænæssas.   (219-23a)

Hrothgar suddenly comes upon the features of Grendel's mere
he has been looking for:

he feara sum   beforan gengde
wisra monna   wong sceawian,
oþ þæt he færinga   fyrgenbeamas
ofer harne stan   hleonian funde,
wynleasne wudu;   wæter under stod
dreorig ond gedrefed.[38]   (1412-17a)

In each case a preceding "flat" piece of narrative,

oð þæt ymb antid   oþres dogores
wundenstefna   gewaden hæfde

and

he feara sum   beforan gengde
wisra monna   wong sceawian,

heightens the moment of sharp recognition. And so it is at all
stages of action. Motivation is a "psychological" reaction. A
Heathobard veteran says to a young warrior:

"Meaht ðu, min wine,   mece gecnawan,
þone þin fæder   to gefeohte bær
under heregriman   hindeman siðe,
dyre iren,   þær hyne Dene slogon,
weoldon wælstowe,   syððan Wiðergyld læg,
æfter hæleþa hryre,   hwate Scyldungas?
Nu her þara banena   byre nathwylces
frætwum hremig   on flet gæð,
morðres gylpeð,   ond þone maðþum byreð,
þone þe ðu mid rihte   rædan sceoldest."[39]   (2047-56)

38. "He went ahead with a few wise men to examine the country, until
suddenly he found mountain trees leaning over a grey rock, an unpleasant
wood; bloody and turbid water lay underneath."

39. "Can you, my friend, recognize the sword which your father wearing
his helmet carried to battle for the last time, beloved blade, when the Danes
killed him, ruled the battlefield, after Withergyld lay dead, after the fall of
heroes, valiant Scyldings? Now here a son of one or another of the slayers

The inception of important action has its mental state:

> Ða com of more   under misthleoþum
> Grendel gongan,   Godes yrre bær;
> mynte se manscaða   manna cynnes
> sumne besyrwan   in sele þam hean.
> Wod under wolcnum   to þæs þe he winreced,
> goldsele gumena   gearwost wisse
> fættum fahne.[40]   (710-16a)

When Beowulf arrives at the barrow where he is to take on the *weard unhiore*, the "horrible guardian," of the treasure,

> Gesæt ða on næsse   niðheard cyning;
> þenden hælo abead   heorðgeneatum,
> goldwine Geata.   Him wæs geomor sefa,
> wæfre ond wælfus.[41]   (2417-20a)

The sad and restless thoughts of the old man approaching death color all the ensuing events. As action proceeds we are kept in constant touch with its mental concomitants. Throughout Beowulf's fight with Grendel's mother we learn about the cave, isolated deep under the water, only as Beowulf sees it:

> Ða se eorl ongeat,
> þæt he in niðsele   nathwylcum wæs,
> þær him nænig wæter   wihte ne sceþede,
> ne him for hrofsele   hrinan ne mehte
> færgripe flodes;   fyrleoht geseah,
> blacne leoman   beorhte scinan.[42] (1512b-17)

---

goes on the floor exulting in the precious things, boasts of the killing and wears the treasure which by right you ought to possess."

40. "Then came Grendel moving from the moor under banks of mist, bearing God's anger; the criminal injurer meant to ensnare one of the human race in the lofty hall. He advanced under the skies until he clearly perceived the wine-hall, the gold-hall of men, decorated with beaten gold."

41. "Then the king brave in battle sat down on the headland, while, generous friend of the Geats, he wished his hearth-companions good fortune. His mind was sad, restless and ready for death."

42. "Then the warrior perceived that he was in some enemy hall or other, where no water harmed him at all and the sudden grip of the flood could not reach him because of the roofed hall; he saw firelight, a brilliant beam of light, shine brightly."

When the hero draws the gigantic sword to deal the blow that will despatch the *mihtig merewif*, he is *aldres orwena*, "despairing of his life" (1565a). Similarly, in his later fight, he and the terrible dragon he has deliberately provoked to mortal combat strike fear into each other on coming face to face:

> æghwæðrum wæs
> bealohycgendra   broga fram oðrum.[43] (2564b–65)

The ending of action too is placed in a mental perspective. Beowulf's fight with Grendel, in which he establishes himself as a hero, finishes with a contrast between Grendel's despair and Beowulf's confidence. Beowulf's exultation at killing Grendel's mother—"secg weorce gefeh" (1569b)—is set off by the total despair of the waiting Danes and by the gloomy feelings of the Geats dispelled only when they see him alive. Beowulf's complex state of mind at his death is surrounded by interconnected attitudes—the grief of Wiglaf; the shame of the traitors; Wiglaf's bitter condemnation of them; the uneasy sadness of Beowulf's people, when, after waiting

> bega on wenum,
> endedogores   ond eftcymes
> leofes monnes[44]   (2895b–97a),

they are brought the news of his death with its grave implications for their future.

Speech, like action, is a "psychological" attribute: to Beowulf on the point of departure, pledging aid and comfort to his grateful host if need arises, Hrothgar replies,

> ne hyrde ic snotorlicor
> on swa geongum feore   guman þingian.[45] (1842b–43)

For "psychological" reasons speech can be preferred to immediate action, however pressing the latter's claims may be. Wiglaf does not rush to the aid of Beowulf, enveloped by the dragon's deadly fire, until he has urged upon his timorous companions their obligations and his own determination; his

---

43. "Each of them intent on destruction felt terror of the other."
44. "expecting both, the last day and the return of the beloved man."
45. "I have not heard a man speak more wisely in so young a life."

action, when it comes, is thus in immediate "psychological" contrast to their inaction. Integrity of thought, word and deed constitutes the whole man. The interplay of states of mind, speech and action is a principal narrative concern.

The "psychological" nexus of the doer communicates with the surrounding world through symbols. The doer recognizes and reacts to tokens around him and himself offers tokens for recognition. The Danes react in the way they do to a second raid by Grendel, because they recognize in it just such a sign: they abandoned sleeping in the hall

> ða him gebeacnod wæs,
> gesægd soðlice   sweotolan tacne
> healðegnes hete.[46]   (140b–42a)

Similar signs, in their various ways, are Beowulf's stature and bearing, *ænlic ansyn*, on his arrival in Denmark; his declaration of intent, *gilpcwide*, which pleases Wealhtheow; the gold-hall, *goldsele gumena*, which Grendel makes for in the night; the horrid, flame-like light, *leoht unfæger*, that shines from Grendel's eyes; the footprints, *feorhlastas*, he leaves when dying; the damaged hall, *bold tobrocen*, which all set to and redecorate; horses and weapons, *wicg ond wæpen*, conferred as a reward of which Beowulf need not feel ashamed; Æschere's head on a cliff by the mere, and Grendel's head carried by the hair, an *egeslic* and *wrætlic wliteseon*, a "terrible" and "amazing spectacle," into the hall where men are drinking; a sword-hilt, *gylden hilt*, relic of the ancient strife of giants against God, which evokes Hrothgar's "sermon"; a dead father's sword, *mece*, before the eyes of the young Heathobard warrior; a cup, *fæted wæge*, stolen to serve as a peace-offering; the dragon's fire, *bryneleoma*, destroying a countryside; and many, many more. The symbols, expressed in traditional language, belong to shared consciousness.[47] They give concentrated form to general experience. The general experience im-

46. "when the hatred of the hall-thane was indicated to them, truly declared by a clear sign."

47. Although they can be misunderstood, as the watching Danes and Geats misinterpreted the blood that rose to the surface of the pool when Beowulf cut off Grendel's head.

plied by setting the main actions of a hero's lifetime successively in a richly enjoyed hall, a difficult and dangerous mere
and a barrow surrounded by *westen*, "desert," is the human
sequence of living, surviving and dying.

The basis of literary form is the agent, not the action: the
cumulative actions of the central personage are the determining factor. The hero constitutes at once the sequence and the
range of interactions explored. The span of the hero is the
span of the poem. (For once, in *Beowulf*, we have an Old
English poem correctly named.) Indeed, in an important sense
the hero *is* the poem, experienced absolutely by us as hearers
and readers. Like seafarers seeing Beowulf's memorial mound
on the clifftop, we have an unrestricted view; we have only an
impersonal narrator for company. Like the mound, the poem
is not devised for observation from any particular direction. It
is simply *aræred geond widwegas*, "raised up throughout far-
extending ways" (as Hrothgar says of Beowulf's renown
[1703b–04a]), in the regions of Germanic and biblical antiquity. Like the mound, the poem sums up a hero's significance.
It too is a *beadurofes becn*, a "sign of a man brave in battle."
It is a token of deeds done. Grendel's hand, arm and shoulder,
Grendel's head and the sword hilt, and the treasure in the
barrow were such tokens, but, unlike any of these, the poem is
a monument to a whole life. It encompasses both incisive action in response to evident need and action arising from a
sense of duty, born of gloomy self-questioning and of proper
pride in past achievements; it admits principles of moral recti-
tude as well as the more dubious force of circumstances; it
accepts that there may be sufficient or insufficient foresight,
sufficient or insufficient capability; it allows for both confidence and fear, even despair; it recognizes that success may be
complete, but eventually corrupt, or partial, but long-lasting
in reputation. It displays a high regard for initiative, daring,
courage, vigor of manhood, self-control and balance of mind,
integrity of word and deed, sympathy, generosity and gratitude, an absence of vindictiveness, loyalty, a sense of social
propriety and of obligations to society, and a proper sense of
human limitations and of dependence on and faith in God. It
shows understanding of those who act criminally, those who

act recklessly, those who act out of strong feelings, those who
delay acting, those who fail to act and those who cannot. It
indicates the frail periphery of human action as well as its
commanding center. The motivation, performance and consequence of actions involve strong personal relationships. Evoca-
tive symbols endow actions with inclusive validity. Powerful
themes of responsibility, judgment and fame are generated.

Hrothgar declares to Beowulf,

> Þu þe self hafast
> dædum gefremed,   þæt þin dom lyfað
> awa to aldre.⁴⁸   (953b–55a)

The poem is the means by which that statement becomes true.
Assimilated verbally into a longeval, collective cultural tradition—just as Beowulf's victory over Grendel is assimilated by
the "guma . . . gidda gemindig" (868)—the reputation of Beowulf's active life takes on a timeless, general existence. The
poetic art by which a *wrætlic* ("wonderful") verbal token for
all time has been fashioned out of the whole of Beowulf's deeds
is assuredly no less worthy than were, we may suppose, the
skill and experience with which his memorial mound of wood
and stone was designed by *foresnotre* ("very clever") *men.*

48. "You yourself have achieved by your deeds that your glory will live for
ever" (Klaeber supplies *dom*).

INDEX

93 — crinkum – crankum